CLOUDED
by
EMOTION

Studies on the
Holy Spirit and Miracles

LANCE MOSHER

Foreword by Kevin L. Moore, PhD

Clouded by Emotion:
Studies on the Holy Spirit and Miracles

Copyright © 2019 Lance Mosher

Edited by Bradley S. Cobb

Cover design by Lance Mosher

Cover background photo by Chuttersnap

ISBN: 978-0-9897041-3-7

In cases where there is emphasis within the Scripture text, the emphasis is the author's.

Some names of the individuals who appear in this work have been changed to protect their rights and privacy.

Lance Mosher BOOKS.com
FOR YOUR JOURNEY

"**Clouded by Emotion** is eminently readable, refreshingly biblical and wonderfully practical. Most of all, it's beautifully God-focused."
—MIKE VESTAL, Preacher

"Many find the topic of the Holy Spirit mysterious and related questions challenging and difficult. With an easy style and expert handling of Scripture, this book will grant truth-seekers of any level a greater understanding of these oft misunderstood topics."
—SERGE SHOEMAKER, Minister

"Lance moves from student to teacher as he tackles the challenging and beautiful topic of the Holy Spirit's actions in our lives—and does so with grace and an open Bible."
—DR. JEREMY JINKERSON, Clinical Psychologist

"**Clouded by Emotion** is very biblical and gets down to the core issues that many worshipers neglect today. The objective truth of God's word is discussed and put first, rather than subjective emotions."
—JAY PAHETOGIA, Evangelist

"This book does an excellent job of explaining a difficult topic in plain, understandable language. I think the use of stories at the beginning of the chapters will help people to see the problems that so many have when it comes to their (mis)understanding of the Holy Spirit."
—MARTIN KLAMM, Missionary

"**Clouded by Emotion** will challenge people to take a serious look at the subject of the Holy Spirit."
—MARK LANCE, Preacher

"Many have written books about the Holy Spirit, but unfortunately few of us turn to the Holy Spirit to see what He says about Himself. Lance has turned the right page… As is typical of the truth, this book will open the eyes of those seeking truth and will disturb the status quo."
—KRISTOPHER SUTTON, Preacher

"This is an outstanding study, and I'm confident it will accomplish much good in the Lord's kingdom."
—DR. KEVIN L. MOORE, Associate Professor of Bible and Missions, Freed-Hardeman University

To my first mentors in the faith:
David Mitchell, Whitney Mitchell, Jovan Payes,
Stan Mitchell, Earl Edwards, Clarence McDowell,
and Kevin Moore

FOREWORD

Beyond the Bible itself, two books every Christian ought to have in his or her personal library are Lance Mosher's *Transformed: A Spiritual Journey* and the current volume. Each will help lay a solid biblical foundation upon which to build and strengthen one's faith, while serving as a valuable resource for outreach and group studies.

In *Clouded by Emotion*, tackling a vast and complex subject, Lance provides reasonably concise, easy-to-understand, biblical explanations of the Holy Spirit and His documented work. Lance does a masterful job confirming biblical authority, while demonstrating how to contextually interpret and apply biblical truth. His careful analysis of Scripture offers sound guidance for the uninformed and corrective instruction for the misinformed. The straightforward approach pulls no punches when challenging subjectivity and confronting error, but it is never demeaning or unkind.

Most chapters begin with a real-life, personal account, making the study practical, meaningful, and applicable. Lance writes with conviction, humility, and concern for the spiritual well-being and eternal destiny of his readers. Study this book with an open Bible and an open heart, and expect a deeper appreciation and clearer understanding of the critical role and efficacy of God's Holy Spirit.

KEVIN L. MOORE, PHD
July 2019

INTRODUCTION

I stood up on the sidewalk, dusted myself off, and looked around to make sure I hadn't left any litter from my lunch break. Adjusting my sunhat, I stepped out of the shade of the pohutukawa tree. I pulled the map out of my pocket, confirming the next house. Approaching number 21, I noticed a van—what New Zealanders call a "people mover"—in the driveway. I climbed the three steps to the front door. There were several pairs of shoes on the landing.

I reached to knock on the door, but it was already open. "Kia ora!" I shouted into the doorway.

"Kia ora!" came the reply. A moment later, a jolly-looking, middle-aged man filled the door frame.

"Hi. My name is Lance. I—"

"Good day, Lance. I'm Tetupuorongo." He stuck out his hand.

I shook it. "Good afternoon, Tetu...Sorry, could you say that one again?"

"Tetupuorongo."

"Tetupu-o," I tried again. There was a moment of silence.

The man grinned. "Ah, I'm just joking! No one calls me by my Cook Island name around here. Call me Danny."

"Hey, I can say that one! But don't worry; I'll work on your Cook Island name."

"That means a lot to me. Thank you. So, what can I do for you, Lance?"

"Well, I had it all planned out what I was going to say, but I've lost the spiel. What I came to offer you was a Bible study."

"Oh?"

"Yes. I love studying the Bible with others, and I'm looking to meet new people today who are interested in the same," I said.

"That sounds great," Danny said. "I'm a deacon at the Victory Apostolic Church. Honestly, I could do with a bit more Bible study. Lately, I've been listening to the Holy Spirit, if you know what I mean."

"I think you're the first churchgoer I've met on your street," I said. "I actually used to be a member of the Apostolic Church in the United States. But what do you mean by listening to the Holy Spirit?"

"Well, you know, when the Spirit speaks to you in your heart, or when you speak in tongues in church. That's what I've really been focusing on. I read the Bible as much as I can, but I haven't studied it much. Come on in!"

Danny showed me to his dining room, which was adjacent to the living room.

"Hey, turn that TV off! We've got a guest!" Danny said to the three people sitting on the couch.

I looked toward the dining table and saw two more people. There were yet another couple of people in the kitchen. And I could hear kids playing in the back bedrooms.

"Big family!" I said. "Congratulations!"

"Yeah. School holidays are nearly over. It'll be a bit more peaceful next week. Have a seat." He gestured to the dining table. "Tea? Coffee?"

* * * * * * *

That was in the summer of 2013, and it was the first of dozens of times I had the privilege of sitting around Danny's dining table. And yes, I soon learned how to pronounce "Tetupuorongo," at least enough for Danny to show great appreciation.[1]

We began studying the basics, like who Jesus is and the authority the Scriptures have in our lives. Because of his influences and experiences, he wanted to spend a lot of time talking about the Holy Spirit and miracles. I was also greatly interested in

---

[1] Te-too-pod-oh-ong-oh

those subjects because of my history in the Apostolic Church, which was before I had studied the Scriptures for myself.[2] But I delayed those subjects for two reasons. First, I wanted to make sure we both agreed that our commitment was to the Scriptures, and not to our feelings or family traditions. Second, I was nervous. I had never done a deep study of what the Scriptures say about the Holy Spirit and miracles. I knew some of the basic information, but I was certainly not ready to lead Bible studies on the subjects. It was time for that to change.

My friend, Stan Mitchell, was once asked, "How does one go about writing a book on a Bible-based subject?" His response? "First, you teach a class on it." I suppose the next logical question to ask is, "How does one go about teaching a class on a Bible-based subject?" You must study it. And to teach it well, a half-hearted study won't do. You must study it deeply.

I began my nearly year-long in-depth study of the Holy Spirit and miracles. Danny was the first person I shared my studies with. Over the next few months, he and I became close friends around open Bibles. We were amazed at how much information about the Holy Spirit there is in the Bible. Danny admitted that prior to our study on the Holy Spirit and miracles from the Scriptures, nearly all of his knowledge on the subject was clouded by his emotions. He was sure the Holy Spirit was something you feel, rather than someone you know. He was sure the Holy Spirit's work in people's lives was more associated with losing control over the body than self-control, which makes up part of the fruit of the Spirit.[3]

After studying the Holy Spirit and miracles from the Scriptures with Danny, I started developing lessons I could teach in a Bible class setting. That later turned into curriculum for a course in a school of preaching. Then it became a sermon series. And now it has become a book. I am still not finished studying.

I assure you the study of the Holy Spirit and miracles is worth your time. It is difficult at times, but not impossible to

---

[2] See my book, *Transformed: A Spiritual Journey.*
[3] See Galatians 5:22–23.

understand.[4] Unfortunately, mankind has turned the Holy Spirit into a controversial subject. And because there are many differing ideas and teachings about the Holy Spirit and miracles today, much of this book must be spent on identifying the false ideas while allowing the Holy Spirit to explain who He is and what He does by studying the Scriptures.

Our Lord says the foremost commandment involves loving the Lord your God with all of your *mind.*[5] Among their many qualities, the Scriptures are logical. Of course, that does not mean all of God's teachings will make perfect sense the first time we read them. When Jesus tried to teach Nicodemus spiritual truths, particularly concerning the new birth (which involves the Spirit), Nicodemus had trouble understanding—at least at first. Then, Jesus asked him:

> *If I told you earthly things and you do not believe, how will you believe if I tell you heavenly things?*
>
> *John 3:12*[6]

When I say the Scriptures work logically, I mean when all teachings and contexts are considered, the words of Scripture are reasonable and noncontradictory. Though the subject of the Holy Spirit is often clouded by emotion, as my friend Danny became well aware, we will approach it by studying the Scriptures with our *minds*, but not, of course, leaving our emotions out of the matter. Let us engage this subject with our entire beings.

> *Jesus answered, "The foremost is, 'Hear, O Israel! The Lord our God is one Lord; and you shall love the Lord your God with all your heart, and with all your soul, and with all your mind, and with all your strength.'"*
>
> *Mark 12:29–30*

Thirteen studies—framed as questions—on the Holy Spirit and miracles lay before you in this book. The answers to these

---

[4] See Ephesians 3:1–5 and 5:15–17.
[5] See Mark 12:30.
[6] Unless otherwise noted, Scripture quotations in this book are taken from the New American Standard Bible® (NASB). In cases where there is emphasis within the Scripture text, the emphasis is the author's.

and other questions can be found within the Scriptures.[7] You do not need a book such as this one to answer them for you. But if you could use some help connecting the dots, perhaps it will be of service. As tempting as it may be, don't skip around in this book at first to jump to answers to specific questions. Instead, read it in order, as the chapters are meant to work sequentially, each chapter assuming knowledge of the previous one. This book has a twofold purpose:

1. To provide non-exhaustive, yet solid, easy-to-understand, scriptural teachings on the person and work of the Holy Spirit.
2. To provide logical tools and information to refute false teachings regarding the person and work of the Holy Spirit.

As we will see, the Holy Spirit is due our reverence, so it should be an utmost priority for us to know the scriptural way to follow Him, believe in Him, approach Him, and teach others about Him. Are you ready to commit to this study? Grab a Bible, and let's dig in.

LANCE MOSHER
August 2019

---

[7] See 2 Timothy 3:16–17 and 2 Peter 1:3.

TABLE OF CONTENTS

1
WHO IS THE HOLY SPIRIT?

"Look, Lance," William said, "I know you have heard a lot of messages out there. But God is not a God of confusion."

"So you've said," I responded.

"Do you know who first said that?" he asked, while finishing up the real estate sign.

After becoming a Christian, I was blessed to land a job as a graphic designer at a local sign shop owned and run by Christians. Conversations like this almost cost me my job at a restaurant where I had worked, but they were encouraged at the sign shop. "No," I admitted. "Who said it?"

"The apostle Paul. And he said it in the context of talking about spiritual gifts from the Holy Spirit."

"Devin and I studied speaking in tongues and stuff last year, but it's still confusing for me. My friends from the Apostolic Church said the other day—"

"Come here and sit down for a moment," William said. "I mean no disrespect, Lance, but maybe that's your problem."

I sat down, glad for the small break. "What is?"

"You listen to your friends too much. And that includes me. It seems you're asking everyone around you questions about the Holy Spirit and miracles, but you're not asking the right person—God."

I was silent. William was right. In the past eleven months, I had studied the Scriptures ten times more than in the previous seventeen years combined, and I still had not searched the Scriptures on this particular topic.

"There's nothing wrong with talking to your friends," William continued. "But it seems, at least in this area, doing so has confused you even more. And God is not a God of—"

"—confusion," I finished.

"It boils down to this. What's going to be your authority in this matter? Your experiences? Your friends' experiences? My answers to your questions? Or God's inspired word?"

I nodded. "Where do I start?"

* * * * * * *

Although nearly a decade passed before I really started to dig, William was right all along. The Scriptures had all the answers I needed. And it didn't require friends, experiences, or preachers to tell me what the truth was. All I had to do was be willing to put forth the effort. That is not to say, of course, that I did not benefit from hearing great sermons and lectures, reading articles and books, and having deep conversations and Bible studies with people who have done much study as well.[1]

Therefore be careful how you walk, not as unwise men but as wise, making the most of your time, because the days are evil. So then do not be foolish, but understand what the will of the Lord is.

Ephesians 5:15–17

for God is not a God of confusion but of peace, as in all the churches of the saints.

1 Corinthians 14:33

The Holy Spirit is mentioned in Scripture over 80 times in the Old Testament, and over 250 times in the New Testament. If you read from the King James Version, many times, God's Spirit is referenced as "the Holy Ghost." For instance, in Matthew 28:19, Jesus tells the eleven to baptize "in the name of the Father, and of the Son, and of the Holy Ghost." However, the New American Standard Bible says, "in the name of the Father and the Son and the Holy Spirit." Most other translations would also say "Holy Spirit." Why the difference?

The words "ghost" and "spirit" have switched basic meanings

---

[1] See closing thoughts and acknowledgements at the end of this book.

since the King James Version was published. In the 1600s, a specter—what we know as a "ghost" today—would have been called a "spirit." Matthew 14:26, in the King James Version, says:

> *And when the disciples saw him walking on the sea, they were troubled, saying, It is a **spirit**; and they cried out for fear.*

The New American Standard Bible says:

> *When the disciples saw Him walking on the sea, they were terrified, and said, "It is a **ghost**!" And they cried out in fear.*

There is no doctrinal difference between the King James Version saying "Holy Ghost" and other translations saying "Holy Spirit." Instead, it is simply an example of how language changes over time.

In a study on the Holy Spirit, it is prudent to begin with His identity, as this will set a foundation for the rest of the studies. The Holy Spirit is the same as "the Spirit of God" (Genesis 1:2) and "the Spirit of Christ" (1 Peter 1:11). The Holy Spirit is a "He." In the upper room, during the same night Jesus would be betrayed, He promised the apostles:

> *But the Helper, the Holy Spirit, whom the Father will send in My name, He will teach you all things, and bring to your remembrance all that I said to you.*
>
> John 14:26

Jesus said to them later that night:

> *But when He, the Spirit of truth, comes, He will guide you into all the truth; for He will not speak on His own initiative, but whatever He hears, He will speak; and He will disclose to you what is to come.*
>
> John 16:13

There are some religious groups who would oppose the idea of God's Spirit having a personhood. Instead, they insist, the Holy Spirit is not alive, but is a nonliving *force*, claiming that the Spirit is simply personified, like wisdom is in Proverbs 8. However, the following Scriptures will show that there is more than simple personification going on.

The Holy Spirit can be blasphemed

Therefore I say to you, any sin and blasphemy shall be forgiven people, but blasphemy against the Spirit shall not be forgiven. Whoever speaks a word against the Son of Man, it shall be forgiven him; but whoever speaks against the Holy Spirit, it shall not be forgiven him, either in this age or in the age to come.

Matthew 12:31–32

The Holy Spirit can be insulted

How much severer punishment do you think he will deserve who has trampled under foot the Son of God, and has regarded as unclean the blood of the covenant by which he was sanctified, and has insulted the Spirit of grace?

Hebrews 10:29

The Holy Spirit can be grieved

Do not grieve the Holy Spirit of God, by whom you were sealed for the day of redemption.

Ephesians 4:30

The Holy Spirit can be lied to

But Peter said, "Ananias, why has Satan filled your heart to lie to the Holy Spirit and to keep back some of the price of the land?"

Acts 5:3

The Holy Spirit can be resisted

You men who are stiff-necked and uncircumcised in heart and ears are always resisting the Holy Spirit; you are doing just as your fathers did.

Acts 7:51

The Holy Spirit has wisdom and intelligence

For who among men knows the thoughts of a man except the spirit of the man which is in him? Even so the thoughts

of God no one knows except the Spirit of God.
    1 Corinthians 2:11[2]

The Holy Spirit speaks with a will and authority
While they were ministering to the Lord and fasting, the Holy Spirit said, "Set apart for Me Barnabas and Saul for the work to which I have called them."
    Acts 13:2[3]

The Holy Spirit radiates goodness
Teach me to do Your will,
For You are my God;
Let Your good Spirit lead me on level ground.
    Psalm 143:10[4]

The Holy Spirit shares in fellowship
The grace of the Lord Jesus Christ, and the love of God, and the fellowship of the Holy Spirit, be with you all.
    2 Corinthians 13:14[5]

How can one say the Holy Spirit is a nonliving force, when Jesus warned people in the first century that their blaspheming of the Holy Spirit was a sin of paramount consequence? The Scriptures also warn against other sins that can be committed against the Spirit. Can one lie to a *force*? Can a nonliving thing be insulted or blasphemed? Technically speaking, yes, but what comes from speaking against, insulting, and lying to the wind or a rock?

Yes, the Holy Spirit has personhood; therefore, we may say He is a person. Of course, by *person*, we do not mean the Holy Spirit is a *human*. What is meant is He is a being with *personality*. Otherwise, how is the apostle Paul able to talk about the "love of the Spirit" (Romans 15:30). And how can Isaiah talk about how God's people grieved the Holy Spirit (Isaiah 63:10), and

---

[2] See also Romans 8:27 and 2 Peter 1:20–21.
[3] See also Matthew 28:19; Acts 16:7; 21:11–14; and 1 Corinthians 12:11.
[4] See also Nehemiah 9:20.
[5] See also Philippians 2:1.

why would Paul warn Christians not to do the same (Ephesians 4:28–31)?

Since the Holy Spirit is a *person*, one that can love and grieve, let us do as Jesus did and use the pronouns, "who" and "He," rather than "it" when referring to God's Spirit. And since the Holy Spirit is not an "it" (i.e. not a "thing"), we would be gravely mistaken if we think the Holy Spirit can be manipulated. We cannot invoke His presence by dimming the lights, playing repetitive music, or turning on a fog machine, as many religious groups are trying today.

A spirit represents life, particularly intelligent life. Humans are created in the image of God. Animals, trees, and arachnids are not.[6] And it is humanity that is given the commandment, "You shall be holy, for I am holy" (1 Peter 1:16). For a human to become holy, he must apply God's word to his life. Then, God will set him apart for divine purposes. To be holy is to be like God.

And as we have been saying all along, perhaps without thinking about it, God's Spirit certainly is *holy*, but not because the Holy Spirit obtained holiness the way we should, but because this is who He is. When Ananias lied about money he donated to the church, Peter said that lying to the Holy Spirit is the same as lying to God.

> But Peter said, *"Ananias, why has Satan filled your heart to **lie to the Holy Spirit** and to keep back some of the price of the land? While it remained unsold, did it not remain your own? And after it was sold, was it not under your control? Why is it that you have conceived this deed in your heart? **You have not lied to men but to God.**"*
>
> Acts 5:3–4

We read about this exchange when the angel announced the coming of Christ to Mary:

> Mary said to the angel, *"How can this be, since I am a virgin?"* The angel answered and said to her, *"The Holy Spirit*

---

[6] See Genesis 1:26–30 and James 2:26.

will come upon you, and the power of the Most High will
overshadow you; and for that reason the holy Child shall
be called the Son of God."
>   Luke 1:34–35

If Joseph were involved in the conception of this child, Jesus
would have truly been the son of Joseph. Instead, since the Holy
Spirit conceived Jesus in Mary's womb, Jesus is the Son of God.
And if the Holy Spirit is not God, then Jesus would be an illegitimate child.

The Holy Spirit shares attributes only God has, and He performs actions only God can do. For instance, in Psalm 139, the
psalmist knew he could not escape Yahweh, the one true God of
the universe, because God's Spirit is omnipresent.[7]

> O LORD [Yahweh], *You have searched me and known me.*
> *You know when I sit down and when I rise up;*
> *You understand my thought from afar.*
> *You scrutinize my path and my lying down,*
> *And are intimately acquainted with all my ways.*
> *Even before there is a word on my tongue,*
> *Behold, O LORD, You know it all.*
> *You have enclosed me behind and before,*
> *And laid Your hand upon me.*
> *Such knowledge is too wonderful for me;*
> *It is too high, I cannot attain to it.*
> *Where can I go from Your Spirit?*
> *Or where can I flee from Your presence?*
> *If I ascend to heaven, You are there;*
> *If I make my bed in Sheol, behold, You are there.*
> *If I take the wings of the dawn,*
> *If I dwell in the remotest part of the sea,*
> *Even there Your hand will lead me,*
> *And Your right hand will lay hold of me.*
>   Psalm 139:1–10

The Holy Spirit is omnipresent, omniscient, and omnipotent

---

[7] "Yahweh," the name of God in the Scriptures, which has been transliterated from the Hebrew *YHWH* (יְהֹוָה) has also been pronounced *Jehovah.*

with God, because the Holy Spirit *is* God. Only God has the quality and ability of truly being in all places at once, knowing all knowable things, and having power over all physical and spiritual things.

QUALITIES AND ABILITIES OF DEITY	ATTRIBUTED TO GOD	ATTRIBUTED TO THE HOLY SPIRIT
Omnipresence Being in all places at the same time.	Jeremiah 23:23–24 Acts 17:24-28	Psalm 139:7–12
Omniscience Knowledge of all that can be known.	Hebrews 4:13 1 John 3:20	1 Corinthians 2:10–11
Omnipotence The power over all physical and spiritual things.	Genesis 28:3; 35:11 1 Chronicles 29:10-13	Romans 15:19
Creation	Genesis 1:1 Ephesians 3:9	Genesis 1:2 Psalm 104:30
Providence	1 Timothy 6:17 James 1:17	Romans 8:26–28
Power of Resurrection	1 Kings 17:21-22 Romans 6:4	Romans 8:11
Power of Salvation from Sin	Romans 6:23 1 Timothy 2:3-4	John 3:5 Titus 3:5
Sanctification	1 Thessalonians 5:23	2 Thessalonians 2:13
Revelation of God's will	Matthew 11:25 2 Timothy 3:16	John 14:26 1 Corinthians 2:10
Eternal	Deuteronomy 33:27	Hebrews 9:14

With these attributes, we see the Holy Spirit was involved in the creation of the heavens and the earth. He is active in the providence of God. He raises the dead. And He provides salvation from sin. He was the power behind the inspiration of prophecy and the Scriptures, resulting in Paul's referencing them as "the Holy Scriptures" (2 Timothy 3:15 NKJV).

If we recognize the deity of the Holy Spirit and the reverence due Him, we will approach our study of Him and His actions carefully, basing our conclusions on the Scriptures which the Spirit Himself has provided. The Holy Spirit, as the Spirit of God, holds authority in my life and yours, and it would be in our eternal best interest to listen to Him.

The study of God, deity (that is, the state of Godhood), and His attributes is a worthwhile and never-ending endeavor, and I certainly will not claim to exhaust the subject in one study, or even a series of studies. Yet God has provided enough information in His word for us to faithfully and reverently approach Him. The Scriptures, as they describe the deity of the Father, the Son, and the Holy Spirit, also describe roles of each person of the one true God. Notice the following roles the Holy Spirit has been, and in some cases is still, involved in.

The Holy Spirit comforts

> *So the church throughout all Judea and Galilee and Samaria enjoyed peace, being built up; and going on in the fear of the Lord and in the comfort of the Holy Spirit, it continued to increase.*
>
> *Acts 9:31*[8]

The Holy Spirit appoints

> *Be on guard for yourselves and for all the flock, among which the Holy Spirit has made you overseers, to shepherd the church of God which He purchased with His own blood.*
>
> *Acts 20:28*[9]

The Holy Spirit guides and directs

> *I have many more things to say to you, but you cannot bear them now. But when He, the Spirit of truth, comes, He will guide you into all the truth; for He will not speak on His*

---

[8] See also John 14:16–17.
[9] See also Acts 13:2 and 1 Corinthians 12:11.

own initiative, but whatever He hears, He will speak; and He will disclose to you what is to come.

John 16:12–13[10]

The Holy Spirit intercedes

In the same way the Spirit also helps our weakness; for we do not know how to pray as we should, but the Spirit Himself intercedes for us with groanings too deep for words; and He who searches the hearts knows what the mind of the Spirit is, because He intercedes for the saints according to the will of God.

Romans 8:26–27

The Holy Spirit searches the depths of God

For to us God revealed them through the Spirit; for the Spirit searches all things, even the depths of God.

1 Corinthians 2:10

The Holy Spirit strengthens

For this reason I bow my knees before the Father, from whom every family in heaven and on earth derives its name, that He would grant you, according to the riches of His glory, to be strengthened with power through His Spirit in the inner man.

Ephesians 3:14–16

The Holy Spirit speaks and teaches

He who has an ear, let him hear what the Spirit says to the churches. To him who overcomes, I will grant to eat of the tree of life which is in the Paradise of God.

Revelation 2:7[11]

The Holy Spirit testifies

When the Helper comes, whom I will send to you from the Father, that is the Spirit of truth who proceeds from the

---

[10] See also Acts 8:29.
[11] See also Matthew 10:20; John 14:26; 16:13; Acts 8:29; 10:19; 13:2–4; and 1 Timothy 4:1.

Father, He will testify about Me.

John 15:26[12]

The Holy Spirit sanctifies and transforms

...according to the foreknowledge of God the Father, by the sanctifying work of the Spirit, to obey Jesus Christ and be sprinkled with His blood: May grace and peace be yours in the fullest measure.

1 Peter 1:2[13]

As these studies unfold, the Scriptures will elaborate on how the Spirit has accomplished some of these tasks and how He is active in the lives of God's people today. For now, seriously consider whether or not you have submitted to the Holy Spirit's will for your life. How can you learn it?

*So we have the **prophetic word** made more sure, to which you do well to pay attention as to a lamp shining in a dark place, until the day dawns and the morning star arises in your hearts. But know this first of all, that no **prophecy of Scripture** is a matter of one's own interpretation, for no prophecy was ever made by an act of human will, but **men moved by the Holy Spirit spoke from God.***

2 Peter 1:19–21

The prophetic word that was spoken long ago, and the rest of the Holy Scriptures, are from the Holy Spirit. If you are not listening to the Scriptures, you are not listening to the Spirit. If you are ignoring the Scriptures, you are ignoring the Spirit's message for you. Are you listening? Are you studying?

---

[12] See also Acts 5:32.
[13] See also Romans 8:13 and 1 Corinthians 6:11.

DISCUSSION QUESTIONS

1. Do the Scriptures describe the Holy Spirit as a nonliving force or a person? How do you know?

2. What are some of the Holy Spirit's qualities? How do those qualities help us understand who He is?

3. How has your view of the Holy Spirit's identity been changed after this study, if at all?

4. Why do you think so many people are confused today about the true nature and work of the Holy Spirit?

5. What stood out to you as particularly interesting or helpful in this chapter?

6. How does this study help you approach God with greater reverence?

*DEEPER
DEVOTION
www.cloudedbyemotion.com*

2

WHERE IS THE HOLY SPIRIT'S AUTHORITY?

As I walked home from the grocery store, the leaves crunched beneath my feet—leftovers from a long winter. I approached my house, and heard faint singing.

"Then I shall bow with humble adoration, and there proclaim, my God, how great Thou art…"

It was Philip, my neighbor, tending his garden.

"Then sings my soul…" I continued with him, which made him pause.

He looked around and found me. His aged face turned into a warm smile. Still crouching over his garden, he said, "Ah, Mr. Lance. I should have known it was you. Say, what did you preach on this Sunday?"

I had to think about that one. I was already deep into the preparations of my next lesson. Then I remembered. "It was an exposition of Romans 5:6–11, where God's love is given to us, even though we were helpless sinners, enemies of God."

"I'm sure it was powerful."

"The power's in the word, Mr. Philip."

"As you say. One day, though, you'll know the power of the Holy Spirit!"

"And one day," I countered, "you'll agree to a Bible study with me."

Standing up, he looked at his watch. "Maybe that day is today. It's almost lunch time. How about I whip up some sandwiches, and we read the Bible together?"

"That sounds great! I'll go home and put these away," I said, holding up the grocery bags. "I'll be back in ten minutes."

Returning, Bible in hand, I knocked on Mr. Philip's screen door.

"Come in!"

After a prayer thanking God for the food, Mr. Philip asked, "How much time do you put into preparing your sermons?"

"It depends, really. I usually start on Monday, working on it when I can for the next few days. It's usually finished by Thursday. That way I can focus on preparing the delivery on Friday."

"Sounds like a lot of wasted time," he said, but not mockingly. He took a bite of his sandwich.

"What do you mean? I like to be careful how I word things, so it's important for me to spend adequate time preparing."

"My pastor doesn't have to prepare a thing when he preaches," he said.

"He doesn't? Explain that one for me." I said, also taking a bite.

"He gets into the pulpit, and the Holy Spirit does the rest. He believes in the power of the Spirit, just as Jesus did."

* * * * * * *

I have since learned the danger of chit-chatting about the Bible, as opposed to opening, reading, and studying the Scriptures. Through subsequent visits, involving *true* Bible study, I learned Mr. Philip was referencing what Jesus promised the apostles on a couple of occasions:

> *But when they hand you over, do not worry about how or what you are to say; for it will be given you in that hour what you are to say. For it is not you who speak, but it is the Spirit of your Father who speaks in you.*
>
> Matthew 10:19–20
>
> *But the Helper, the Holy Spirit, whom the Father will send in My name, He will teach you all things, and bring to your remembrance all that I said to you.*
>
> John 14:26

It will be our task in this chapter to understand these

promises and others in their contexts. I once believed the Bible to be a magical book that I could pick up, open to a random spot, and point to a verse to find my "message" of the day. But the Scriptures are not a collection of pithy sayings for us to simply copy and paste onto inspirational posters. For us to approach them as such would be an insult to God's Spirit. All Scripture was written in particular times to specific audiences, and every verse has a context—surrounding verses that help us understand what is going on, just like everything you and I say. We would not appreciate it if someone took our words out of context and misapplied them. How much more should we revere God when approaching His word?

To paint the context of the above passages, we must go back to the beginning. As the creator of the universe, God holds all authority over all things.

> *In the beginning God created the heavens and the earth. The earth was formless and void, and darkness was over the surface of the deep, and the Spirit of God was moving over the surface of the waters. Then God said, "Let there be light"; and there was light.*
>
> *Genesis. 1:1–3*

The apostle Paul told the people of Athens:

> *The God who made the world and all things in it, since He is Lord of heaven and earth, does not dwell in temples made with hands; nor is He served by human hands, as though He needed anything, since He Himself gives to all people life and breath and all things.*
>
> *Acts 17:24-25*

God is high above all else, and He needs nothing from us. He created us and gave us all we need to live lives of joy. Instead of fulfilling His purposes, we have taken things into our own hands, and we have fallen into sin. Because of His love, to address our sin problem, God gave His Son,

> *who, although He existed in the form of God, did not regard equality with God a thing to be grasped, but emptied Himself, taking the form of a bond-servant, and being*

made in the likeness of men.

Philippians 2:6-7

Jesus taught all of His disciples to submit to the Father and to revere His name. He taught them:

Pray, then, in this way:
"Our Father who is in heaven,
Hallowed be Your name."

Matthew 6:9

Not only are disciples to submit to the Father, but Jesus Himself also submitted to the will of the Father while on the earth, famously praying, "My Father…not as I will, but as You will" (Matthew 26:39).

In the same night Jesus offered that fervent prayer to the Father, He explained to His disciples:

These things I have spoken to you while abiding with you. But the Helper, the Holy Spirit, whom the Father will send in My name, He will teach you all things, and bring to your remembrance all that I said to you.

John 14:25-26

But I tell you the truth, it is to your advantage that I go away; for if I do not go away, the Helper will not come to you; but if I go, I will send Him to you.

John 16:7

Jesus promised these men that after He departed them, He would send to them the Helper, the Holy Spirit. The Spirit's task would be to teach them all things, bringing to their memories everything Jesus had taught them. Why would that be important? Jesus was hours away from His redemptive work—the purpose for His coming. He was going to be killed for sinners at the hands of sinners, be buried in a tomb not His own, and raised victorious over death and him who has "the power of death, that is, the devil" (Hebrews 2:14). Forty days later, Jesus would leave the earth and the company of the apostles, but not before giving them this commandment:

Go therefore and make disciples of all the nations,

baptizing them in the name of the Father and the Son and the Holy Spirit, teaching them to observe all that I commanded you; and lo, I am with you always, even to the end of the age.

Matthew 28:19–20

Jesus was leaving them with the enormous task of making disciples of all the nations and teaching them to observe *all* He had commanded them. Could you imagine that? They had traveled far and wide with Him for three years or so, hearing Him teach countless messages and watching Him perform countless miracles, on occasion even being granted the same power themselves. Now, it was going to be their job to do the same—to teach all people all He had commanded.

Relatively speaking, it would be easy for us to teach all of His commandments, because we have the completed and confirmed New Testament that provides everything God found worth preserving from Jesus and His messengers. But these men that Jesus had recently commissioned had the task to do it without access to the written New Testament! Cue the Holy Spirit. Jesus had promised them the night before His death:

But the Helper, the Holy Spirit, whom the Father will send in My name, He will teach you all things, and bring to your remembrance all that I said to you.

John 14:26

It must have been a huge relief for the apostles upon remembering this promise. How many of us can say we have never been negatively affected or never made a serious blunder because of our fallible memories? Are you thankful the men entrusted with the soul-saving gospel did not have to rely on their memories and experiences, but instead, were granted the inspiration of the Holy Spirit?[1] In Acts 1, Jesus told these men that they would be

---

[1] The apostles did utilize their personal memories and experiences while writing (see 2 Peter 1:16–18 and 1 John 1:1–4), but this was usually to make an important point about what Jesus had taught them. For example, Peter's point in reminiscing was that his experiences were not the authority; the Holy Spirit's provided Scriptures were (see 2 Peter 1:19–21). The Holy Spirit guided them into the truth of these matters and reminded them of the important details.

His witnesses throughout the world. A few days later in Acts 2, they received the baptism with the Holy Spirit—a subject which will be explored in a later chapter of this book. With the power of the Holy Spirit, the apostles preached the first gospel message regarding the death, burial, and resurrection of Jesus. They surely would have spoken from the heart, but more importantly, they spoke the message of the Holy Spirit. Jesus' promise was being fulfilled—The Holy Spirit taught them all things and brought to their memories all Jesus had taught them.

Yahweh, the God of heaven and earth, has all authority. Jesus, when He came to this earth, subordinated Himself to the Father. Before Jesus left the earth, He said two things to the apostles regarding authority:

1. "All authority has been given to Me in heaven and on earth" (Matthew 28:18).
2. "All things that the Father has are Mine; therefore I said that He [the Holy Spirit] takes of Mine and will disclose it to you" (John 16:15).

What does this say about the Holy Spirit's authority? It says He has the authority of God in your life and mine. But God chose for there to be an order. When Jesus was on the earth, He submitted to the Father's authority, and He taught His disciples to do the same. After the atoning work was done, and Jesus was raised from the dead, He claimed all authority had been given to Him. He had previously explained to the apostles, however, that they had not received all of God's message yet. Instead, the Holy Spirit would take what had been given to Jesus and relay it to the apostles (and later, the New Testament prophets, as described in Ephesians 2:19–3:5). These men would then relay it to the entire world, first through verbally preaching the message, then recording it into what we know as the New Testament. Jesus told them before His death:

I have many more things to say to you, but you cannot bear them now. But when He, the Spirit of truth, comes, He will guide you into all the truth; for He will not speak on His own initiative, but whatever He hears, He will speak; and He will disclose to you what is to come. He will glorify Me,

*for He will take of Mine and will disclose it to you. All
things that the Father has are Mine; therefore I said that
He takes of Mine and will disclose it to you.*

John 16:12–15

Jesus promised to deliver the remaining part of His message
through the Holy Spirit. In the above passage, the Holy Spirit is
referred to as "the Spirit of truth," relating the Holy Spirit to God
"who cannot lie" (Titus 1:2). All words that proceed from the
Spirit are truth. That is how the apostle Paul is able to say:

*If anyone thinks he is a prophet or spiritual, let him recog-
nize that the things which I write to you are the Lord's commandment.*

1 Corinthians 14:37

How does this promise affect us today? First, a warning: the
promises Jesus gave in Matthew 10:19–20 and John 14–16 are
among the most misapplied passages of all Scripture. When
reading the passages out of context, they are easy to misuse. Jesus said the Holy Spirit will provide "*you* in that hour what *you*
are to say" and "teach *you* all things, and bring to *your* remembrance all that I said to *you*." If we, like Mr. Philip and his
preacher, are not careful, we may assume Jesus was speaking directly to *us* when He said "you." There are at least two questions
we should always have in the back of our minds when approaching Scripture, which in most cases, we ask without thinking:

1.   Who is speaking?
2.   To whom is that person speaking?

On these occasions, context tells us Jesus was speaking to the
apostles. In Matthew 10, it was when He sent them out to preach
for the first time. In John 14–16, it was on the eve of His crucifixion. In John 13, Jesus shared the Passover meal with His disciples in the upper room. It was there He also shared unleavened
bread and the fruit of the vine with them, calling the elements
His body and His blood. He washed their feet, predicted Judas'
betrayal, and predicted His own death. Once Judas left the room,
Jesus began comforting, warning, and instructing the remaining
eleven apostles. In the beginning of chapter 14, some of the

apostles spoke up with questions, but the rest of chapters 14–17 are Jesus' words, chapter 17 being His longest recorded prayer in Scripture.

Since Jesus was speaking directly to the apostles when He promised the inspiration of the Holy Spirit, it would be an abuse of Scripture to jump straight to a personal application of this passage, believing the Holy Spirit will directly teach *me* all things. First, I should ask how Jesus' words affected and applied to the original audience. Only after answering that question can I then ask, "How does this affect or apply to me today?"

In Acts 1, Jesus told the apostles this promise would allow *them* to be His witnesses and carry out the commandment to teach the world. They began fulfilling that commandment on the day of Pentecost in Acts 2 when Jews from all over the world assembled in Jerusalem. The apostles continued to preach Jesus' words throughout the first century by the inspiration of the Holy Spirit.

The apostle Paul writes regarding the miracle of Holy Spirit inspiration and revelation:

> *Yet we* [the apostles and prophets of Jesus] *do speak wisdom among those who are mature; a wisdom, however, not of this age nor of the rulers of this age, who are passing away; but we speak God's wisdom in a mystery, the hidden wisdom which God predestined before the ages to our glory; the wisdom which none of the rulers of this age has understood; for if they had understood it they would not have crucified the Lord of glory; but just as it is written, "Things which eye has not seen and ear has not heard, and which have not entered the heart of man, all that God has prepared for those who love Him." For to us God revealed them through the Spirit; for the Spirit searches all things, even the depths of God. For who among men knows the thoughts of a man except the spirit of the man which is in him? Even so the thoughts of God no one knows except the Spirit of God. Now we have received, not the spirit of the world, but the Spirit who is from God, so that we may know the things freely given to us by God, which things we also*

speak, not in words taught by human wisdom, but in those taught by the Spirit, combining spiritual thoughts with spiritual words.

1 Corinthians 2:6–13

The apostle Paul claims the words he spoke were the hidden wisdom of God revealed through the Spirit. How do *we* know that? We read it in the New Testament. Not only did the Lord's apostles and prophets verbally communicate the Holy Spirit's inspired message, but they also recorded it. To teach people distantly, they began writing letters to churches and individual Christians. A letter from a true prophet or apostle of the Lord would have held as much authority as their verbal words. How much authority was that? Remember Jesus' promise to them:

All things that the Father has are Mine; therefore I said that He [the Holy Spirit] takes of Mine and will disclose it to you [apostles and prophets].

John 16:15

When the Holy Spirit provided a message through the apostles and prophets, He was doing so with the authority of God. Consequently, anyone who has ever claimed to have been a prophet or apostle of God has claimed his or her messages were from God, and disobedience to those messages would be sin. True prophecies are not the prophet's message, but God's message.

But know this first of all, that no prophecy of Scripture is a matter of one's own interpretation, for no prophecy was ever made by an act of human will, but men moved by the Holy Spirit spoke from God.

2 Peter 1:20–21

The prophets who delivered God's message were His vessels. They had no business inserting their own interpretations or making things up from their imaginations[2], because it was not their message they were delivering—it was the Spirit's message.

---

[2] Instead of "one's own interpretation" in this passage, the NET Bible says, "the prophet's own imagination."

God expects us to handle the delivered word with respect, so much so that tampering with it will result in condemnation.

I testify to everyone who hears the words of the prophecy of this book: if anyone adds to them, God will add to him the plagues which are written in this book; and if anyone takes away from the words of the book of this prophecy, God will take away his part from the tree of life and from the holy city, which are written in this book.

Revelation 22:18–19

After using Apollos and himself as examples of how God's word is spread, enters into someone's heart, and produces fruit, Paul had this to say:

Now these things, brethren, I have figuratively applied to myself and Apollos for your sakes, so that in us you may learn not to exceed what is written, so that no one of you will become arrogant in behalf of one against the other. For who regards you as superior? What do you have that you did not receive? And if you did receive it, why do you boast as if you had not received it?

1 Corinthians 4:6–7

By the time 1 Corinthians was written, Paul had begun making arguments for the sufficiency of Scripture, and he said so to a congregation of Christians that was blessed with a variety of spiritual and miraculous gifts of the Holy Spirit, including prophecy, tongues, and supernatural knowledge. In effect, he said to them, "If it is written, that is that. No need to add more." Even today, what should we expect of the one who does add more? Thinking he has more to say than the Holy Spirit does, he boasts in his arrogance. This is why adding to or taking away from the word of God is so condemning.

The Scriptures are not the Holy Spirit. The Scriptures are not God. However, the Scriptures are how God's Holy Spirit has chosen to deliver the message of life and godliness to us today and for all generations since the apostles.

After the resurrection, Christ appeared to the apostles, including Thomas, who proclaimed, "My Lord and my God!" (John 20:28).

> *Jesus said to him, "Because you have seen Me, have you believed? Blessed are they who did not see, and yet believed."*
>
> John 20:29

Are you and I among those who believe, though we have not seen His resurrected body? If so, how do we account for that? In the next two verses, John says this about his gospel account:

> *Therefore many other signs Jesus also performed in the presence of the disciples, which are not written in this book; but these have been written so that you may believe that Jesus is the Christ, the Son of God; and that believing you may have life in His name.*
>
> John 20:30–31

The Lord proclaims that His word is sufficient to develop saving faith in an individual. Since His miracles were preserved for us, we do not need to personally witness the miracles of Christ and His apostles to believe and obey Jesus. Both the Holy Spirit and the apostles serve as witnesses to the fact Jesus is the risen Christ.[3] Their testimony is sufficient.

> *…and though you do not see Him now, but believe in Him, you greatly rejoice with joy inexpressible and full of glory, obtaining as the outcome of your faith the salvation of your souls.*
>
> 1 Peter 1:8–9

In the book of Ephesians, Paul explains God's revealed mystery to the Christians, namely that Gentiles are now brought near to God through the blood of Jesus Christ and into His body, the church.

> *For this reason I, Paul, the prisoner of Christ Jesus for the sake of you Gentiles—if indeed you have heard of the stewardship of God's grace which was given to me for you; that*

---

[3] See John 15:26–27; Acts 1:8 and 5:32.

*by revelation there was made known to me the mystery, as I wrote before in brief. By referring to this, **when you read you can understand** my insight into the mystery of Christ, which in other generations was not made known to the sons of men, as **it has now been revealed to His holy apostles and prophets in the Spirit.***

Ephesians 3:1–5

Paul had a message, revealed in the Spirit, that the Christians would be able to understand. How could they do so? By reading what he had written to them. The Holy Spirit has chosen to reveal God's mystery, which had been withheld for many generations, through the writings of the New Testament. Are you thankful for your access to the New Testament Scriptures?

Likewise, when John was exiled to the island Patmos, Jesus had messages to give to the seven churches of Asia. He delivered the messages by revealing them to John in the Spirit, and John was instructed to write the messages down and deliver them to the Christians.

I, John, your brother and fellow partaker in the tribulation and kingdom and perseverance which are in Jesus, was on the island called Patmos because of the word of God and the testimony of Jesus. I was in the Spirit on the Lord's day, and I heard behind me a loud voice like the sound of a trumpet, saying, "Write in a book what you see, and send it to the seven churches: to Ephesus and to Smyrna and to Pergamum and to Thyatira and to Sardis and to Philadelphia and to Laodicea."

Revelation 1:9–11

What unfolds in the next two chapters of Revelation are the messages Jesus had for these Christians. Each message includes this commandment: "He who has an ear, let him hear what the Spirit says to the churches" (2:7, 11, 17, 29; 3:6, 13, and 22). As in the original audience's case, when reading Scripture, which has been delivered through the Holy Spirit, we are hearing what the Spirit says.

What conclusion have we come to? Where is the Holy Spirit's

authority? How do Jesus' promises to the apostles affect us today? The Holy Spirit has expressed His authority through words. God the Father had a message He gave to Jesus, and Jesus delivered that message to the apostles and prophets through the Holy Spirit, telling them:

> *But when He, the Spirit of truth, comes, He will guide you into all the truth; for He will not speak on His own initiative, but whatever He hears, He will speak; and He will disclose to you what is to come. He will glorify Me, for He will take of Mine and will disclose it to you. All things that the Father has are Mine; therefore I said that He takes of Mine and will disclose it to you.*
>
> *John 16:13–15*

The apostles and prophets—the ones Jesus gave these promises to—received God's word by inspiration, and they delivered it first by preaching to their first-century audiences, and then by recording the Holy Spirit's authoritative message in the Scriptures. The Lord preserved those words for even us to read today, so we too can hear what the Spirit says to the churches. Delivery of the Old Testament Scriptures also worked through inspiration of the Holy Spirit.

How do those promises apply to us? When we open the Scriptures, and we allow them to work in our lives, the Holy Spirit does amazing things. Our souls can be saved, and we are equipped for every good work. In other words, the Spirit gave knowledge and words to the apostles, who then wrote down what the Spirit revealed, and we share in that knowledge as we read, study, and apply those things which the Spirit had recorded.

> *Therefore, putting aside all filthiness and all that remains of wickedness, in humility receive the word implanted, which is able to save your souls. But prove yourselves doers of the word, and not merely hearers who delude themselves.*
>
> *James 1:21–22*

All Scripture is inspired by God and profitable for teaching, for reproof, for correction, for training in righteousness; so that the man of God may be adequate, equipped for every good work.

2 Timothy 3:16–17

Let us hold the word of God, the authority of the Holy Spirit, as our standard. Religious experiences may be nice, but they are secondary at best to the confirmed, unchanging word of God.

DISCUSSION QUESTIONS

1. It is clear that not all who profess to believe in the God of the Bible teach the same things. Since God is not the author of confusion, what do these differences suggest?

2. Did the apostles have to depend on their memories when Jesus told them to teach all nations all He had commanded? Why or why not?

3. Why was it important for Jesus to send the Helper to the apostles once He returned to His Father?

4. Why are the promises Jesus gave in Matthew 10:19–20 and John 14–16 among the most abused passages of all Scripture?

5. If Scripture equips us for every good work, what else is needed for us to understand God's will?

6. What stood out to you as particularly interesting or helpful in this chapter?

7. How does this study help you approach God with greater reverence?

*DEEPER
DEVOTION
www.cloudedbyemotion.com*

3

WHAT ARE MIRACLES AND
THEIR QUALITIES?

My friend and I sat with four inmates around a stainless steel table in the inner room of the local jail. I had begun a jail ministry, and things were starting to pick up speed. I was developing friendships with many of the inmates with whom I was permitted to study the Bible. We were listening to Raymond's story of how he became incarcerated.

Raymond leaned in for effect. The rest of us followed suit subconsciously. We could tell he was getting to the good part of the story. "So, the four of us ran to the truck. It was an S-10—you know how small the cabs are in those trucks."

The rest of us nodded, not wanting to interrupt his story with words.

"So, I jumped into the back of the truck, while the other three climbed into the cab. James was driving. He floored it to get a head start away from the cops. Everything was cruisy, until James took a quick turn onto a dirt road. He lost control. The truck swerved—first left, then right, then it tipped. I was thrown from the back of the truck, and I hit the ground before the truck finished tipping." He pointed to a scar on his forehead.

No one spoke.

Raymond continued. "I was about three feet from the truck when it finally toppled. It then rolled—the first of three times—but it *jumped* over me. It's crazy. I thank God for it every day. I should have died right then and there. But God must have thought ten years in the slammer would be punishment enough. The cops said I was lucky to leave with my life. Apparently, the people who were hired to survey the wreckage said it was like one in a million I survived. *Luck?* I call it a *miracle.*"

The rest of us exhaled and leaned back in our chairs. Our eyes settled on nothing in particular as we reflected on how close it was that we never would have known Raymond.

"Are you sure it was a *miracle?*" I asked Raymond after a minute of silence.

"Without a doubt. There's no way I would have survived without God's help."

"Oh, I don't doubt God was involved," I said. "I'm just wondering if we should look at this event as a miracle."

"How else would we see it?" Raymond asked. "Like I said, it was one in a million I even survived, much less walked away with only a gash on my forehead."

"But that's the point. It all happened with natural laws in place. There was a one in a million chance that the centrifugal force and gravity would place you in just the spot that the truck would skip while rolling, all while preserving your bones and organs. I'm thankful God was there for you. He surely protected you, but He utilized physics to do so. It's not like He made you fly home. Or it's not like you died, were buried, and then were resurrected a few days later."

* * * * * * *

Raymond and I continued to peacefully discuss the difference between our understandings of how the word *miracle* should be used. Looking back, I could have been more sensitive to Raymond. After all, he had just shared with us what was likely his most life-changing moment. That probably was not the best time to disagree over definitions. But I am grateful he shared his story with us. I went home that night and started studying this subject in greater depth.

The word *miracle* has been used in many contexts and in many ways. If someone survives a horrible car crash, it's quickly labelled a miracle. When a baby is born, people thank God for His miracle. When a man is offered a job a week before his family is evicted from their home, it's called a miracle. In addition to all of that, when Christ raised the dead and restored withered limbs, those were also called miracles. Are all of these events in the same category?

According to Scripture, the answer is both *yes* and *no*. When people of Scripture saw amazing things happen—both natural and supernatural—they credited God's power.[1] In the New Testament, the word "power" is usually translated from the Greek word *dynamis* (δύναμις), where we receive our English word *dynamite*.

This word is used over one hundred times in the New Testament. In a few cases, it is a reference to the authority God has granted to rulers of men (i.e. political power).[2] However, in most cases, this word is used for the power that inherently belongs to God. The fact that astonishes the people of God in Scripture, and should drive us to our knees today, is that the Creator of the universe decided to share that power with His creation! In the majority of cases, Scripture explains He has done so through "works of power"—signs, wonders, and miracles.

> *For I will not presume to speak of anything except what Christ has accomplished through me, resulting in the obedience of the Gentiles by word and deed, in the **power** of **signs and wonders**, in the **power of the Spirit**; so that from Jerusalem and round about as far as Illyricum I have fully preached the gospel of Christ.*
>
> *Romans 15:18–19*

When God acts on earth, whether through natural means or supernatural means, it is certainly powerful. Even that which we refer to as "natural laws" came about by supernatural means.

> *He* [Jesus] *is the image of the invisible God, the firstborn of*

---

[1] Although the word *supernatural* is often associated with superstition, what is meant in this book by *supernatural* are events that do not occur through the natural order and laws of the universe which God Himself has established, thereby events that supersede nature.

[2] See John 19:10–11 and Romans 13:1–2, which says earthly political power comes from God; and see 1 Corinthians 15:24 and Ephesians 1:21, where earthly kingdoms' power (*dynamis*) is referenced.

all creation. *For by Him all things were created, both in the heavens and on earth, visible and invisible, whether thrones or dominions or rulers or authorities—all things have been created through Him and for Him. He is before all things, and in Him all things hold together.*

Colossians 1:15–17

When a child is conceived, God is involved in some supernatural way in order to provide the human's spirit.[3] Only God has the authority and power to grant life. Therefore, when a baby is conceived and is born, give God the praise. As the giver of life, God also has the authority to take life. Therefore, give God the glory for His mercy when a life is spared, as it was in Raymond's case.

If we are going to be consistent with the way Scripture references God's powerful working through men, then we will not be so quick to label God's power through natural means as *miracles*. A situation where someone who is in grave danger is saved at the last minute by a fortuitous encounter may be one in a million, but it does not require defiance of gravity, time, space, or any other such limitation. Application of a paramedic's or a doctor's skills to save a life is amazing, and God answers prayers in that way today, but He does so through His natural laws. When someone slowly recovers from cancer, God is to be credited, yet we will see that does not match up with a scriptural understanding of a miracle. Upon close investigation of God's work through the natural laws He established in the beginning, we learn the Scriptures would not label those as signs, wonders, or miracles. Instead, those words are reserved for describing the supernatural powers of God, sometimes being performed through the hands of men.

Though God has worked wonders by Himself many times and many ways directly on the world (for instance: creation itself, the parting of the Red Sea, and stopping the flow of the Jordan River), what we will primarily focus on in this chapter are the times God worked through humans, providing them with

---

[3] See Ecclesiastes 12:7; Zechariah 12:1; and James 2:26.

supernatural power.

Signs are established to point to something. Jesus' miraculous signs, for example, point to His authority, His deity. More on that in the next chapter. Wonders are almost always referenced and performed alongside signs. They are supernatural abilities or events that cause people to marvel, or *wonder*. Miracles include signs and wonders and all of the powerful works of God through people.[4] For the sake of the cohesion of this book, when miracles are referenced, signs and wonders are also included.

In the example above (Romans 15:18–19), when Paul was granted the ability to perform signs and wonders, he gave credit to the Holy Spirit's power within him. In reality, the ancient people of God did not have a clear division in mind between "natural" and "supernatural" the way we do today. They simply saw that God is the orchestrator of the universe, and they gave Him praise over everything, and so should we. We should not assume that if something happens "naturally," then God was not involved. We must not be so quick to hold back our praises.

> *When I consider Your heavens, the work of Your fingers,*
> *The moon and the stars, which You have ordained;*
> *What is man that You take thought of him,*
> *And the son of man that You care for him?*
> *Yet You have made him a little lower than God,*
> *And You crown him with glory and majesty!*
> *You make him to rule over the works of Your hands;*
> *You have put all things under his feet,*
> *All sheep and oxen,*
> *And also the beasts of the field,*
> *The birds of the heavens and the fish of the sea,*
> *Whatever passes through the paths of the seas.*
> *O LORD, our Lord,*
> *How majestic is Your name in all the earth!*
> *Psalm 8:3–9*

If the psalmist can praise God over something as "natural" as

---

[4] See Acts 2:22; 8:13; 2 Corinthians 12:12; and Hebrews 2:4.

shepherding a sheep in a field, then so can I. But to call a sheep in a field, or the flight of a bird, or a school of fish a sign, wonder, or miracle would be to use the terms differently than Scripture uses them.

WHAT ARE MIRACLES?

When Jesus came to the earth, from beginning to end of the gospel accounts, the authors emphasize He came performing miracles in public. Some of those miracles included healing the sick by speaking to them and even raising the dead. During His triumphal entry into Jerusalem, the Scriptures say:

> *As soon as He was approaching, near the descent of the Mount of Olives, the whole crowd of the disciples began to praise God joyfully with a loud voice for all the miracles which they had seen.*

> *Luke 19:37*

Raising the dead? Healing sick people with your voice? That's not natural. That is supernatural. Although there are some good and wordy definitions of the word *miracle* out there, the simplest way to define true miracles in a biblical way is: "A supernatural event or work by the power of God."

If that is the case, how do we approach God's decision to bless us through natural means?

> *But I say to you, love your enemies and pray for those who persecute you, so that you may be sons of your Father who is in heaven; for He causes His sun to rise on the evil and the good, and sends rain on the righteous and the unrighteous.*

> *Matthew 5:45*

When reading this passage, it is typical for readers to assume the sunshine represents good things, and the rain represents bad things. However, in an agricultural environment in which Jesus originally spoke this, sunshine and rain were both good things.

Some have called God's blessings through natural means "providence," the idea that God *provides* through natural laws. When good and natural things happen to people, it's God who is doing it, but not every time God blesses us is it miraculous. In fact, even in the biblical account, the times God blessed people naturally far outweigh the times He intervened supernaturally with miracles (which were primarily only during three ministries: Moses and Joshua; Elijah and Elisha; and Jesus and the apostles). Out of the thousands of years of history the Scriptures cover, only about two hundred years feature times of miraculous events.

By emphasizing a scriptural definition of God-given miracles, we do not mean to take away from God's glory when He works even today through His providence. Take a deep breath. Can you breathe? That's a good thing; therefore, that's a gift from God. He provided that breath just for you, "for in Him we live and move and exist" (Acts 17:28)! Pause right now and thank Him for that.

Now that the distinction between God's powerful working through providence and through miracles has been made, let us explore our second question.

WHAT ARE THE QUALITIES OF MIRACLES?

The first time the word *miracle* is used in the English Scriptures is in Exodus 3:20, in reference to the signs and wonders God would perform through Moses and Aaron in order to show Israel and Egypt that Yahweh is God. One of the notable miracles is mentioned in Exodus 7:9:

> *When Pharaoh speaks to you, saying, "Work a miracle," then you shall say to Aaron, "Take your staff and throw it down before Pharaoh, that it may become a serpent."*

God was providing supernatural power to His messengers to prove they came with the message and authority of the Almighty. Throwing a staff to the ground is natural. But for it to then turn into a real serpent, that is supernatural. When Aaron did throw down his staff before Pharaoh, and it turned into a real serpent, as opposed to some form of trickery, how can that be explained apart from the power of God?

Miracles were of God

The creator of the universe, the one who set natural things in order, is the only one with the authority to work outside of natural laws. True miracles testify of God's power and love. There are some cases in the Scriptures where wonders are credited to humans and spiritual beings without God's authority. However, in those cases, they are called "secret arts" (Exodus 7:11), "false wonders" (2 Thessalonians 2:9), or "signs and wonders" of "false Christs and false prophets" (Matthew 24:24).

Miracles worked outside the laws of nature

As amazing as some natural events are on earth, only those events that can be accounted for exclusively by God's supernatural means should be called miracles.

Miracles were instantaneous and fully effective

With miracles, there was no need for calling a doctor. There was no gradual improvement. There was no recovery time. And there was no post-procedure follow-up. Apart from a single account where Jesus performed a miracle in two parts for a specific purpose in Mark 8:22–26, all miracles in the Scriptures had their complete effect immediately.

*Moved with compassion, Jesus touched their eyes; and **immediately** they regained their sight and followed Him.*

Matthew 20:34

*Taking the child by the hand, He said to her, "Talitha kum!" (which translated means, "Little girl, I say to you, get up!"). **Immediately** the girl got up and began to walk, for she was twelve years old. And immediately they were completely astounded.*

Mark 5:42

*And He stretched out His hand and touched him, saying, "I am willing; be cleansed." And **immediately** the leprosy left him.*

Luke 5:13

*Jesus said to him, "Get up, pick up your pallet and walk." **Immediately** the man became well, and picked up his* *pallet and began to walk.*

> *John 5:8–9*

Miracles were observable and undeniable by the public

When teaching with authority, Jesus backed up His authority with the power of God, manifested in His miracles.

> *Now there was a man of the Pharisees, named Nicodemus, a ruler of the Jews; this man came to Jesus by night and said to Him, "Rabbi, we know that You have come from God as a teacher; for no one can do these signs that You do unless God is with him."*
>
> *John 3:1–2*
>
> *But many of the crowd believed in Him; and they were saying, "When the Christ comes, He will not perform more signs than those which this man has, will He?"*
>
> *John 7:31*

Some people today claim faith is a requirement for a miracle to occur. For instance, in so-called "faith healing" meetings, if someone is not healed, the person's lack of faith is frequently blamed. In Scripture, faith was sometimes a working part of a miracle, but not always. For instance, in John 9, Jesus publicly healed a blind man who did not even know who Jesus was at the time, much less had faith in Jesus and His abilities. The city quickly learned of the miracle, and the authorities got involved.

In Acts 3, Peter and John performed a miracle for a crippled man who was asking for money in Jerusalem at a temple gate. As far as we know, the first time he heard about the power of Jesus was when Peter and John miraculously healed him. The Scriptures say this man was "lame from his mother's womb" (Acts 3:2). His legs had never been used. Those who witnessed this miracle might have seen atrophied legs immediately filled with muscles before he began "walking and leaping and praising God" (Acts 3:8).[5] The public miracle caused such a public

---

[5] See also Jesus' healing of a man's withered hand in Luke 6:6–11, where the Pharisees and scribes—those trying to trap Him—were "watching Him closely" while He performed the miracle.

response, the Jewish council arrested Peter and John and brought them in for questioning.

> *And seeing the man who had been healed standing with them, they had nothing to say in reply. But when they had ordered them to leave the Council, they began to confer with one another, saying, "What shall we do with these men? For the fact that a noteworthy miracle has taken place through them is apparent to all who live in Jerusalem, and we cannot deny it.*
>
> Acts 4:14-16

Even the enemies of Christianity were unable to deny the fact a notable miracle had taken place in public.

> *There he found a man named Aeneas, who had been bedridden eight years, for he was paralyzed. Peter said to him, "Aeneas, Jesus Christ heals you; get up and make your bed." Immediately he got up. And all who lived at Lydda and Sharon saw him, and they turned to the Lord.*
>
> Acts 9:33-35

Miracles like this were not done in private church buildings for the faithful. They were done in the open where even those who were antagonistic toward Jesus and His gospel could witness them. When open-minded people saw them, the only proper response was to believe and praise God. True miracles are of God, they worked outside the laws of nature, they were instantaneous and fully effective, and they were observable and undeniable by the public.

If you believe in the miracles of the Scriptures, do you have the same response those of the first century did? Admittedly, we might not be driven to leap and praise God the way an instantly healed man did. However, the fact that God shared such gifts with people to accomplish such great things gives us a glimpse into His love for us. If He provided healing for physical illnesses, how much more does He care for our spiritual state?[6]

---

[6] This is evident when four friends brought a paralyzed man to see Jesus for healing, and Jesus showed the priority of forgiveness over physical healing, forgiving the man of his sins before healing his paralysis. See Mark 2:1-12.

To anyone who believes modern-day churches are performing miracles today, let me encourage you to take a step back, and truly analyze what is going on. Do these so-called miracles align with the qualities of miracles in the Scriptures? I know our observation can be clouded by emotion and make this a difficult task. But compare what you think you see with the genuine miracles of the Scriptures. Are you truly witnessing things like this?

- Turning water into wine (John 2:1–11)
- Calming a storm by commanding it to be quiet and still (Matthew 8:26; Mark 4:39; John 8:22–25)
- Immediate cleansing of leprosy (Matthew 8:2–3)
- Feeding thousands with a single serving (Matthew 14:15–21; 15:32–38)
- Walking on water (Matthew 14:24–29; John 6:19)
- Restoring maimed or severed body parts (Luke 22:50–51; Matthew 15:30–31; Mark 3:1–5)
- Raising the dead (Luke 7:12–17, 22; John 12:1; Acts 9:36–42; 20:9–11)
- Complete, immediate healing of adults lame from birth (Acts 3:2–10; 14:8–10)
- Complete, immediate healing of adults blind from birth (John 9:1–11, 32)
- Every sick person in a given area healed (Matthew 8:16; 9:35; 12:15; Luke 4:40; 6:17–19; Acts 5:16)
- Speaking a language never studied that unbelievers understand (Acts 2:1–11)
- Causing an enemy of the truth to instantly go blind (Acts 13:11)
- Observable by the public, including even the enemies of God's word (John 9; Acts 3–4)

How many of these have you personally witnessed? Not stories or alleged events, but personally witnessed? Many today claim the ability to work miracles, including "holy men" of the Hindu religion, pagan witch doctors, self-proclaimed psychics, spiritualists, leaders of the Latter-day Saints, Roman Catholic priests, alleged "faith healers," sorcerers, witches, and so on.

Should they all be seen as God's servants? If you hear people claiming to be able to perform miracles, ask them why they do so, and challenge them to perform a *real* miracle. Can the people who claim to have miraculous power of the Holy Spirit measure up?

No, so-called miracles happening in modern churches today are an insult to God's Holy Spirit. These "faith healers" are mocking Jesus. Many claim they are performing miracles to help the sick. If so, why not perform real miracles in hospitals today? Ask Jesus the same question, and the truth is, though He did help many who were suffering, helping people was not the primary reason for His miracles. If so, He would have healed all of the sick, raised all of the dead, and fed all of the hungry. Why did Paul leave behind Trophimus, his sick companion in the faith?[7] Why did he not simply heal him? As noble as it would have been to do so, there was something more important the Holy Spirit was accomplishing.

> *How will we escape if we neglect so great a salvation? After it was at the first spoken through the Lord, it was confirmed to us by those who heard, God also testifying with them, both by signs and wonders and by various miracles and by gifts of the Holy Spirit according to His own will.*
>
> *Hebrews 2:3–4*

Take the time to thank God for the genuine miracles He has performed since creating the universe. They were not performed to "show off." They had a primary purpose. We will study that purpose in the next chapter.

---

[7] See 2 Timothy 4:20.

DISCUSSION QUESTIONS

1. What are the similarities and differences between God's power in providence and His power in miracles?

2. What were some of the qualities of miracles?

3. Why was it important that miracles were performed in public?

4. Can people perform true miracles today? How do you know?

5. What are the differences between stories of alleged miracles today and the miracles of God in the Scriptures?

6. What stood out to you as particularly interesting or helpful in this chapter?

7. How does this study help you approach God with greater reverence?

DEEPER DEVOTION
www.cloudedbyemotion.com

4

WHAT WERE THE PURPOSES OF MIRACLES?

"Lance, do you believe God is still working miracles today?" Sunil asked me, as he put more putty on his knife. He and I had both been asked by a mutual friend to help with renovating his house.

"That's a great question!" I said. "I've been studying that topic from the Scriptures a lot lately. What do you think a miracle is?"

He wore a thoughtful expression. He was granted more time to think while the saw was being used right outside the window. "Well," he began, as things quieted down. "I think a miracle is when God makes something happen that can't be explained by natural means. You know, supernatural stuff—healing the blind, walking on water."

"That's a pretty good definition. Do you think Christians are able to perform miracles today?" I asked.

"Why not?" he said. "I mean, I haven't personally witnessed any, but who's to say believers in other parts of the world aren't doing them?"

I thought for a second. "Even in Bible times, why did God give people miracles?"

"Hmm. I haven't really thought about that," he admitted. "I guess to give God the glory and to help people. Right?"

* * * * * * *

The idea of miracles personally fascinates me. To think God has provided power that belongs to Him alone to His lowly, fallen creation sends me to my knees. We are surely not worthy. But why would He do such a thing? The answer to this question is vitally important, though few people are asking it, much less studying the Scriptures to answer it.

What seems to be the first obvious answer is that God gave miraculous abilities to people in order to help others. In some cases, Jesus compared His casting out of evil spirits and healing of lame, crippled, mute, and deaf people to a normal person that gives his livestock water when they are thirsty or lifting them out of a ditch if they have fallen.[1] In those cases, doing so would be "to do good" (Matthew 12:12). But doing good to others was not the primary purpose for miracles.

While doing good by freeing people from illnesses and demons, the Scriptures also explain that the miraculous works of Jesus and His apostles were a direct assault on the power and bondage of Satan. When sin entered the world, man was cast out of the Garden, thereby being removed from the presence of God and the tree of life. Life was replaced by death, and the effects of Satan have been evident ever since.[2] When people witnessed Christ's raising Lazarus from the dead, effectively reversing the outcome of sin, people witnessed "the glory of God" (John 11:40).

This was a prelude to something much greater—the resurrection of Jesus. Lazarus was raised, but he eventually died once more. However, Jesus rose never to taste death again. This same resurrection is offered to all who trust in Him.

> *But now Christ has been raised from the dead, the first fruits of those who are asleep. For since by a man came death, by a man also came the resurrection of the dead. For as in Adam all die, so also in Christ all will be made alive.*
>
> *1 Corinthians 15:20–22*

John tells us, "The Son of God appeared for this purpose, to destroy the works of the devil" (1 John 3:8).

> *Therefore, since the children share in flesh and blood, He*

---

[1] See Mark 3:1–6; Luke 13:10–17; and 14:1–6.
[2] See Genesis 2:15–17; 3:22–24; Romans 5:12–18; and 6:23.

> *Himself likewise also partook of the same, that through death He might render powerless him who had the power of death, that is, the devil.*
>
> *Hebrews 2:14[3]*

When Jesus rose from the dead, He proved the power He has to destroy the strength of Satan. He has offered that same resurrection to us, so long as we follow the evidence where it leads—to a complete submission to the Lord and His revealed will. This brings us to the primary purpose of miracles. Notice the result of Jesus' resurrection of dead Lazarus.

> *When He had said these things, He cried out with a loud voice, "Lazarus, come forth." The man who had died came forth, bound hand and foot with wrappings, and his face was wrapped around with a cloth. Jesus said to them, "Unbind him, and let him go."* **Therefore many of the Jews who came to Mary, and saw what He had done, believed in Him.**
>
> *John 11:45*

As noted in the previous chapter, the first time the word *miracle* appears in the English Scriptures is in the context of Moses and Aaron's works in Egypt. Moses was commissioned to go to Egypt to speak to the Israelites and announce their coming liberation. But Moses had reservations.

> *Then Moses said, "What if they will not believe me or listen to what I say? For they may say, 'The LORD has not appeared to you.'" The LORD said to him, "What is that in your hand?" And he said, "A staff." Then He said, "Throw it on the ground." So he threw it on the ground, and it became a serpent; and Moses fled from it. But the LORD said to Moses, "Stretch out your hand and grasp it by its tail"—so he stretched out his hand and caught it, and it became a staff in his hand— "that they may believe that the LORD, the God of their fathers, the God of Abraham, the God of*

---

[3] The Greek word for *power* in this verse is not *dynamis*, as previously explored, but it is *kratos* (κράτος), a reference to strength.

Isaac, and the God of Jacob, has appeared to you."
Exodus 4:1–5

The purpose for Moses' miracles was so the people he appeared to would believe he came as a true messenger of God. Likewise, after God performed a miracle of resurrection through the prophet Elijah, the previously unbelieving widow of Zarephath said, "Now I know that you are a man of God and that the word of the LORD in your mouth is truth" (1 Kings 17:24).

Jesus came as a prophet with an authoritative message. He claimed to His audience, "unless you believe that I am He, you will die in your sins" (John 8:24). But anyone can, and many have, come into a city, claimed to be the Christ from God, and demanded belief. How are we to know which one truly is the anointed one of God?

They went into Capernaum; and immediately on the Sabbath He entered the synagogue and began to teach. They were amazed at His teaching; for He was teaching them as one having authority, and not as the scribes. Just then there was a man in their synagogue with an unclean spirit; and he cried out, saying, "What business do we have with each other, Jesus of Nazareth? Have You come to destroy us? I know who You are—the Holy One of God!" And Jesus rebuked him, saying, "Be quiet, and come out of him!" Throwing him into convulsions, the unclean spirit cried out with a loud voice and came out of him. They were all amazed, so that they debated among themselves, saying, "What is this? A new teaching with authority! He commands even the unclean spirits, and they obey Him."
Mark 1:21–27

Jesus did not only claim to have authority; He also proved His authority with His miracles. As Nicodemus admitted that he knew Jesus was a teacher from God because of the signs He performed, we too can recognize the truth about Jesus by His miracles. In fact, the apostle John tells us that is why God had the miracles recorded in the gospel accounts.

*After eight days His disciples were again inside, and Thomas with them. Jesus came, the doors having been shut, and stood in their midst and said, "Peace be with you." Then He said to Thomas, "Reach here with your finger, and see My hands; and reach here your hand and put it into My side; and do not be unbelieving, but believing." Thomas answered and said to Him, "My Lord and my God!" Jesus said to him, "Because you have seen Me, have you believed? Blessed are they who did not see, and yet believed." Therefore many other signs Jesus also performed in the presence of the disciples, which are not written in this book; **but these have been written so that you may believe that Jesus is the Christ, the Son of God; and that believing you may have life in His name**.*

   John 20:26–31

Biblical faith is not blind. It is based on evidence. What does the evidence point to? When people truly study the evidence for Christianity, they come away knowing the miracles in the Bible were true, historical events. After all, if the first verse in the Bible is true, then all things are possible. We come away from the Scriptures believing that God truly sent those who performed the recorded miracles. Jesus says the blessed ones are those who believe without having seen. No, I have not personally seen Jesus' resurrected body, but examining the evidence causes me to believe in His resurrection, and because of that miracle (and others), I believe He is my Lord and my God.

> *…and though you have not seen Him, you love Him, and though you do not see Him now, but believe in Him, you greatly rejoice with joy inexpressible and full of glory, obtaining as the outcome of your faith the salvation of your souls.*
>
> *1 Peter 1:8–9*

What was the primary purpose of providing people with the ability to perform miracles, signs, and wonders? There were times God helped people through miracles. There were times God did not explain Himself for why He performed particular miracles.[4] But when all is considered, the consistent primary reason God gives for having provided His messengers the ability to work wonders was to confirm that the messengers and their message come with His authority.

After His resurrection, Jesus told His disciples, "Go into all the world and preach the gospel to all creation. He who has believed and has been baptized shall be saved; but he who has disbelieved shall be condemned" (Mark 16:15–16). It was imperative that the hearers of the gospel message believed what they heard. Otherwise, they would be eternally condemned. But again, anyone can claim to have a message from God. How were the first audiences of the gospel to know the apostles' words were truly from God? Keep in mind this was before their words were confirmed in writing in what we call the New Testament. A few verses later, we read:

> *And they went out and preached everywhere, while the Lord worked with them, and confirmed the word by the signs that followed.*
>
> *Mark 16:20*

When God sent a messenger with a new message, He sent signs that confirmed the message. On the other hand, when people had access to a confirmed message, miracles were neither needed nor provided. Such was the case with the rich man in the story of the rich man and Lazarus. The formerly rich man was in torment, and he begged Abraham for a miracle of resurrection to convince his family to change their lives.[5] Then, we read:

> *But Abraham said, "They have Moses and the Prophets; let them hear them." But he said, "No, father Abraham, but if someone goes to them from the dead, they will repent!" But he said to him, "If they do not listen to Moses and the Prophets, they will not be persuaded even if someone rises from the dead."*
>
> *Luke 16:29–31*

---

[4] See 2 Kings 6:1–7 and Acts 9:36–40.
[5] See Luke 16:27–28.

The formerly rich man was asking for confirmation of a message that was already available and confirmed. Therefore, a miracle was neither needed nor provided. Such is the case throughout Scripture. Miracles were never the end in mind. They were a means to an end, which was to convince people to believe in God's word. Once that was accomplished, miracles had fulfilled their purpose.

It is also helpful to note that John's gospel refers to Jesus' miracles as *signs*.

> *This beginning of His signs Jesus did in Cana of Galilee, and manifested His glory, and His disciples believed in Him.*
>
> *John 2:11*

Signs are meant to point to something. Jesus' signs point to His authority and His deity. The purpose God recorded the signs in the Scriptures was so the reader would believe in Him to whom the signs point. If Jesus were still performing such signs on the earth (whether through apostles and prophets or not), there would be no reason to have the signs recorded. What do we have in place of the signs? The confirmed Scriptures. When the Scriptures are available to read, the emphasis is placed there, not on the miracles.

> *For this reason we must pay much closer attention to what we have heard, so that we do not drift away from it. For if the word spoken through angels proved unalterable, and every transgression and disobedience received a just penalty, how will we escape if we neglect so great a salvation? After it was at the first spoken through the Lord, it was confirmed to us by those who heard, God also testifying with them, both by signs and wonders and by various miracles and by gifts of the Holy Spirit according to His own will.*
>
> *Hebrews 2:1–4*

Today, we have access to the Old and New Testaments, the completed Scriptures, confirmed by the Holy Spirit. Jude tells us this faith, the system of doctrine from the Scriptures, has been "once for all handed down to the saints" (Jude 3).[6] Should we expect God to send more miracle-workers to confirm a message that has already been confirmed for centuries? The apostle Paul's warnings of deceitful workers may also apply to those who would claim such things.

> *For such men are false apostles, deceitful workers, disguising themselves as apostles of Christ. No wonder, for even Satan disguises himself as an angel of light. Therefore it is not surprising if his servants also disguise themselves as servants of righteousness, whose end will be according to their deeds.*
>
> *2 Corinthians 11:13–15*

We must beware. There are those out there who serve Satan. They disguise themselves as righteous religious leaders. Jesus warned His disciples of the first century:

> *For false Christs and false prophets will arise and will show great signs and wonders, so as to mislead, if possible, even the elect.*
>
> *Matthew 24:24*

Simply because a miracle is claimed, and even some people genuinely believe it, does not mean God is the one behind the so-called power. Of course, not everyone claiming to be performing these signs, wonders, or miracles is doing so with the intent to deceive. Indeed, some believe they are serving God. Jesus warns:

> *Not everyone who says to Me, "Lord, Lord," will enter the kingdom of heaven, but he who does the will of My Father who is in heaven will enter. Many will say to Me on that day, "Lord, Lord, did we not prophesy in Your name, and in Your name cast out demons, and in Your name perform many miracles?" And then I will declare to them, "**I never knew you; depart from Me, you who practice lawlessness.**"*
>
> *Matthew 7:21–23*

---

[6] See also Galatians 1:6–12.

Can you imagine living your life in complete confidence that you're on your way to spend eternity with God, yet hear the words of Jesus on the day of judgment, "I never knew you; depart from Me"? What is it that will provide these people with the false expectation of inheriting the kingdom of heaven? They will simply call Jesus "Lord" (without living it out[7]), and they will believe they are performing miracles in the name of God. We must do all we can to ensure this prophecy will not apply to us.

A popular term in religion today is "faith healing." As popular as it is, that phrase never appears in the Scriptures. I have had many conversations with people who claim genuine miracles and "faith healings" have taken place in their assemblies. But my question is this: What are the purposes of those alleged miracles? Are the purposes consistent with the purposes of miracles in the Scriptures, primarily to confirm the messenger and his message are from God? If so, are the messages consistent with everything that has already been revealed in the Scriptures? And if so, is the audience's faith in God's word so weak that they must witness miracles in the twenty-first century to believe the revealed will of God? The apostle Paul wrote in 1 Corinthians that it is the immature, childish Christian who needs miracles and signs to keep his faith afloat.

> *Love never fails; but if there are gifts of prophecy, they will be done away; if there are tongues, they will cease; if there is knowledge, it will be done away. For we know in part and we prophesy in part; but when the perfect comes, the partial will be done away. When I was a child, I used to speak like a child, think like a child, reason like a child; when I became a man, I did away with childish things.*

> *1 Corinthians 13:8–11*

We will examine this text in much greater depth in a later chapter. The point now is the apostle looked forward to the day when the word was completed and confirmed and the church would mature so as not to need miracles. Jesus said, "An evil and adulterous generation craves for a sign" (Matthew 12:39).

---

[7] See Luke 6:46–49.

Many enjoy the hype of so-called miracles in their assemblies, claiming they produce faith in the congregation. But I side with the Holy Spirit, who said through Paul:

> *So faith comes from hearing, and hearing by the word of Christ.*
>
> *Romans 10:17*[8]

Have the authentic miracles of God, which are recorded in Scripture, fulfilled their purpose in your life? Do you "believe that Jesus is the Christ, the Son of God; and that believing you may have life in His name" (John 20:31)?

---

[8] The Greek word for *word* in this passage is *rhēma* (ῥῆμα), which is a reference to the spoken, or uttered, word. When the Scriptures are verbally preached, they are capable of developing faith within the hearer. Moreover, when the utterance of Christ's story—His gospel—is told to someone, it is enough to cause even a witness to a genuine miracle fall on his face to worship God (see 1 Corinthians 14:24–25).

DISCUSSION QUESTIONS

1. What were the purposes of miracles? What was the primary purpose?

2. Why were Jesus' signs recorded in the Scriptures?

3. When is a miracle neither needed nor provided?

4. If Jesus or His servants were performing true miracles, signs, and wonders today, what would be unnecessary? Why?

5. What is one way Satan deceives people today that was discussed in this chapter?

6. What stood out to you as particularly interesting or helpful in this chapter?

7. How does this study help you approach God with greater reverence?

*DEEPER
DEVOTION
www.cloudedbyemotion.com*

5

WHAT WAS BAPTISM WITH THE HOLY SPIRIT?

I leaned over to point to a word in Alicia's Bible. "In Mark 9:1, Jesus said the kingdom would come with *what*?"

Alicia was a new Christian, hungry for the word and determined to "grow in the grace and knowledge of our Lord and Savior Jesus Christ" (2 Peter 3:18).

"Power," she said. "The kingdom would come with *power*."

"Right. Now, let's turn to Acts 1:4–8." We read the passage together before I asked, "Here, Jesus told the apostles the baptism with the Holy Spirit was *what* by the Father?"

"*Promised* by the Father."

"That's right. And then, what did they ask Jesus about?"

"The kingdom! I think I'm starting to get it," Alicia said. "It's kind of like these two 'p' words—*promise* and *power*—are things to look out for when the kingdom comes."

"Yeah, I like the way you put that," I said. "So, as we continue in our study, let's look for those two words. Now, read the next verse."

After reading, she said, "Ah! The promise is what *provides* the power!"

"And context tells us the promise is…?"

"The Holy Spirit," she said.

"Yes! And specifically, regarding *what* in verse five?"

She saw it right away. "Baptism with the Holy Spirit. So, when the baptism with the Holy Spirit happened, they would receive power, and then it would be time for them to start preaching. Right?"

"You got it! With that in mind, let's read Luke 24:46–49. Let's also remember Luke wrote the book of Acts as well. The end of Luke 24 overlaps the events of the beginning of Acts chapter 1. Look for the 'p' words in this passage."

* * * * * * *

The baptism with the Holy Spirit—especially in connection with the kingdom of God and the preaching of the gospel—is one of my favorite subjects to study with others. When I was a young Christian, the subject was mysterious, because I had heard a lot of people talk about their experiences. However, when I studied the subject from the Scriptures in their contexts, it made a lot more sense to me, and I was able to see it much less through the eyes of confused religious people clouded by emotion, and much more through the eyes of God.

Pick up the gospel account of Mark and begin reading. One of the first promises you will come across is:

> *And he was preaching, and saying, "After me One is coming who is mightier than I, and I am not fit to stoop down and untie the thong of His sandals. I baptized you with water; but He will baptize you with the Holy Spirit."*
>
> *Mark 1:7–8*

I remember reading this for the first time wondering what it meant that Jesus would baptize with the Holy Spirit. That is the first point I want to make in this study. A basic reading renders this truth: When this promise was to be fulfilled, it would be Jesus doing the baptizing. The rest of the questions we may have about baptism with the Holy Spirit can be answered as easily, again, if we read the passages on the subject in the overall New Testament context.

Here are the questions we will allow the Scriptures to answer in this chapter:

1. What was baptism with the Holy Spirit?
2. Who received baptism with the Holy Spirit?
3. What were the purposes of baptism with the Holy Spirit?
4. Is the baptism with the Holy Spirit for today?

WHAT WAS BAPTISM WITH THE HOLY SPIRIT?

The word *baptism* comes from the Greek word *baptisma* (βάπτισμα), which is defined as "plunging, dipping, washing, water-right, baptism."[1] Biblically speaking, to be baptized means to be immersed. For example, after Jesus' baptism in water, He came "up immediately from the water" (Matthew 3:16). Jesus was immersed in water. When Philip baptized a man with water, the Scriptures say:

> *And he ordered the chariot to stop; and they both went down into the water, Philip as well as the eunuch, and he baptized him.*
>
> *Acts 8:38*

The eunuch was immersed in water. The Scriptures describe those who have been baptized as people who have been "buried" (Romans 6:4; Colossians 2:12). To be baptized with water means to be fully covered or immersed in water. Since the Scriptures describe the topic at hand as baptism *with the Holy Spirit,*[2] then it must have been the idea of being fully immersed with the Holy Spirit, which, as the following Scripture indicates, resulted in the manifestation of His power.

> *And suddenly there came from heaven a noise like a violent rushing wind, and it filled the whole house where they were sitting. And there appeared to them tongues as of fire distributing themselves, and they rested on each one of them. And they were all filled with the Holy Spirit and began to speak with other tongues, as the Spirit was giving them utterance.*
>
> *Acts 2:2–4*

Later in this chapter, Peter describes this event as something Jesus was accomplishing.

> *Therefore having been exalted to the right hand of God,*

---

[1] Danker, Frederick W., Walter Bauer, William F. Arndt, and F. Wilbur Gingrich. *Greek-English Lexicon of the New Testament and Other Early Christian Literature.* 3rd ed. Chicago: University of Chicago Press, 2000, 165.

[2] Some translations say, "baptism *of* the Holy Spirit."

> *and having received from the Father the promise of the*
> *Holy Spirit, He* [Jesus] *has poured forth this which you*
> *both see and hear.*
>
> Acts 2:33

From heaven, Jesus poured out the Holy Spirit upon these men. This baptism with the Holy Spirit gave them the ability to speak with other tongues. In this account, it was an amazing spectacle experienced by the faithful and witnessed by those who were not yet believers in the gospel. This did not happen in a private assembly, but among the people who were guilty of the crucifixion.

> *This Jesus God raised up again, to which we are all wit-*
> *nesses. Therefore having been exalted to the right hand of*
> *God, and having received from the Father the promise of*
> *the Holy Spirit, He has poured forth this which you both*
> *see and hear. For it was not David who ascended into*
> *heaven, but he himself says: "The Lord said to my Lord, 'Sit*
> *at My right hand, until I make Your enemies A footstool*
> *for Your feet.'" Therefore let all the house of Israel know for*
> *certain that God has made Him both Lord and Christ—*
> *this Jesus whom you crucified.*
>
> Acts 2:32–36

What was the baptism with the Holy Spirit? It was an immersing in the Holy Spirit and His power on select groups of people in specific moments in history for specific purposes.

WHO RECEIVED BAPTISM WITH THE HOLY SPIRIT?

John the Baptist promised Jesus would baptize with the Holy Spirit. This was a future event from John's perspective. And it was still a future event after Jesus' resurrection, while He was still on the earth.

> *The first account I composed, Theophilus, about all that*
> *Jesus began to do and teach, until the day when He was*
> *taken up to heaven, after He had by the Holy Spirit given*
> *orders to the apostles whom He had chosen. To these He*
> *also presented Himself alive after His suffering, by many*

> *convincing proofs, appearing to them over a period of forty*
> *days and speaking of the things concerning the kingdom of*
> *God. Gathering them together, He commanded them not*
> *to leave Jerusalem, but to wait for what the Father had*
> *promised, "Which," He said, "you heard of from Me; for*
> *John baptized with water, but* **you will be baptized with**
> **the Holy Spirit not many days from now.**"
>
> Acts 1:1–5

We see no record in the gospel accounts—Matthew, Mark, Luke, or John—of the baptism with the Holy Spirit, and here, barely over a week before Pentecost, Jesus told His apostles that His promise of the baptism with the Holy Spirit was finally coming "not many days from now."

A few verses later, Judas was replaced. The last verse in Acts 1 reads:

> *And they drew lots for them, and the lot fell to Matthias;*
> *and he was added to the eleven apostles.*
>
> Acts 1:26

Verse and chapter breaks were added to the biblical text by men over a thousand years after the New Testament was completed. The original reader would neither have consciously nor subconsciously placed a break between what we know as chapters 1 and 2. It is important we include this verse in our reading of the account of Acts 2, because verses 1–4 of chapter 2 reference "they" and "them." If we are not careful, we could assume those pronouns reference the 120 in the middle of chapter 1, or even the thousands of Jews in chapter 2. But the antecedent of "they" and "them" in Acts 2:1–4 is "the apostles" in Acts 1:26.

In the beginning of Acts 1, Jesus promised the apostles they would receive the baptism with the Holy Spirit soon. In the beginning of Acts 2, that promise was fulfilled, which is the first time the Scriptures record the baptism with the Holy Spirit. In this context, Peter claimed it was a fulfillment of a prophecy in Joel 2.

> *…but this is what was spoken of through the prophet Joel:*
> *"'And it shall be in the last days,' God says, 'that I will pour*

> *forth of My Spirit on all mankind; and your sons and your daughters shall prophesy, and your young men shall see visions, and your old men shall dream dreams; even on My bondslaves, both men and women.'"*

> *Acts 2:16–17*

This pouring forth of God's Spirit was to happen "on all mankind." To me, the natural understanding of "all mankind" is "every person everywhere." However, that is not what we see in the Scriptures moving forward. Though Peter says Joel's prophecy was being fulfilled, and that God's Spirit was being poured out on "all mankind," we do not see the baptism with the Holy Spirit happen for every person everywhere in Scripture. In fact, we do not see it again until seven to ten years later in Acts 10.

One way to look at this is that perhaps Peter does not mean that all mankind would receive the baptism with the Holy Spirit, but that God would offer His Spirit to all mankind in some way. Later in the book of Acts, the Holy Spirit empowers some people to perform signs and wonders, certain sons and daughters to prophesy, and select people to see visions without having received the baptism with the Holy Spirit.[3] Additionally, and apart from providing miraculous works, God's Spirit is offered to "every person everywhere," though not every person accepts God's offer. More on that in later chapters.

Another way to look at "all mankind" is that it may simply mean "both Jews and Gentiles." To a Jewish audience in the first century, there were two major groups of people: Jews and Greeks, or Jews and Gentiles.[4]

> *Or is God the God of Jews only? Is He not the God of Gentiles also? Yes, of Gentiles also, since indeed God who will justify the circumcised by faith and the uncircumcised*

---

[3] See Acts 6:8; 16:6–10; and 21:7–14.

[4] Jews (Aramaic for "Judean") were those from the physical nation of Israel. They could trace their physical ancestry back to Abraham (see John 8:31–38). Gentiles were those from all other nations.

through faith is one.

Romans 3:29–30

To a Jewish mindset, to say God's Spirit would be offered to all mankind may not have necessarily meant "every single person." Instead, it could have meant "to both the Jews and the Gentiles." It was Jewish people who received the baptism with the Holy Spirit in Acts 2. What was left of all mankind? The Gentiles.

Put down this book, and take a moment to read all of Acts 10 and 11 together. Up until this point, the gospel of Jesus had not been preached to uncircumcised Gentiles. An angel then visited Cornelius, a Gentile and a devout man of Caesarea. The angel told him God had noticed his devotion and would send him a preacher of the gospel. The next day, the Lord showed to Peter it was time to teach the gospel to Gentiles, as there was no longer a separation of people in the sight of God, since the Law of Moses, which served as a wall between the two people groups, had been broken down.[5]

> *On the following day he* [Peter] *entered Caesarea. Now Cornelius was waiting for them and had called together his relatives and close friends.*
>
> *Acts 10:24*
>
> *While Peter was still speaking these words, the Holy Spirit fell upon all those who were listening to the message. All the circumcised believers who came with Peter were amazed, because the gift of the Holy Spirit had been poured out on the Gentiles also. For they were hearing them speaking with tongues and exalting God. Then Peter answered, "Surely no one can refuse the water for these to be baptized who have received the Holy Spirit just as we did, can he?" And he ordered them to be baptized in the name of Jesus Christ. Then they asked him to stay on for a few days.*
>
> *Acts 10:44–48*

In the next chapter, Peter's fellow Jewish preachers required

---

[5] See Ephesians 2:11–22.

him to give an account for himself. They did not know it was acceptable to take the gospel to all nations. Peter tells them:

> *"And as I began to speak, the Holy Spirit fell upon them just as He did upon us at the beginning. And I remembered the word of the Lord, how He used to say, 'John baptized with water, but you will be baptized with the Holy Spirit.' Therefore if God gave to them the same gift as He gave to us also after believing in the Lord Jesus Christ, who was I that I could stand in God's way?" When they heard this, they quieted down and glorified God, saying, "Well then, God has granted to the Gentiles also the repentance that leads to life."*

> *Acts 11:15–18*

The baptism with the Holy Spirit was not an every day, every disciple experience. In fact, it is not mentioned once between Acts 2 and Acts 10, and the New Testament's timeline shows us seven to ten years passed between those two chapters. For Peter's Jewish friends to understand what Peter witnessed in Cornelius' house, Peter did not say, "You know, what happens to all Jewish believers," or "What happened to the people of such-and-such city last week." Instead, Peter had to relate it to the events found all the way back in Acts 1 and 2. The Gentiles were baptized with the Holy Spirit and filled with the Holy Spirit's power for specific purposes. Therefore, the prophecy had been fulfilled.

I have heard many claim the baptism with the Holy Spirit is available to all disciples today, but that clearly is not the case. There are only two times in all of Scripture the baptism with the Holy Spirit took place, Acts 11:16 being the last verse in Scripture that explicitly references it.

Baptism with the Holy Spirit was given in specific moments in history for specific purposes. Who received baptism with the Holy Spirit? The twelve Jewish apostles in Acts 2 and the Gentiles in Cornelius' house in Acts 10. If there were ever any others,

Scripture does not mention the events.[6] To say not every disciple received or receives the baptism with the Holy Spirit is not to say every disciple did not or does not have the Holy Spirit (this will be discussed much more in later studies).

WHAT WERE THE PURPOSES OF BAPTISM WITH THE HOLY SPIRIT?

When Jesus promised the apostles they would soon be baptized with the Holy Spirit, He said to them:

> ...but you will receive power when the Holy Spirit has come upon you; and you shall be My witnesses both in Jerusalem, and in all Judea and Samaria, and even to the remotest part of the earth.
>
> Acts 1:8

The power from the baptism with the Holy Spirit obviously had to do with taking the gospel to all nations. Jesus told them to wait in Jerusalem until this promise was fulfilled.

> ...and He said to them, "Thus it is written, that the Christ would suffer and rise again from the dead the third day, and that repentance for forgiveness of sins would be proclaimed in His name to all the nations, beginning from Jerusalem. You are witnesses of these things. And behold, I am sending forth the promise of My Father upon you; but you are to stay in the city until you are clothed with power

---

[6] It is possible the apostle Paul also received the baptism with the Holy Spirit, though it is not recorded in Scripture. Perhaps Paul was baptized with the Holy Spirit for some of the purposes discussed later in this chapter. Paul had the gift of tongues, which the other apostles received when they were baptized with the Holy Spirit (see 1 Corinthians 14:18). He did not receive that gift or his commission to preach the gospel by the laying on of the other apostles' hands. To the contrary, Paul explains, "For I would have you know, brethren, that the gospel which was preached by me is not according to man. For I neither received it from man, nor was I taught it, but I received it through a revelation of Jesus Christ" (Galatians 1:11–12). Since men were not involved in Paul's commission to preach the gospel, he may have been baptized with the Holy Spirit.

from on high."
   Luke 24:46–49

When it was time for the apostles to preach the gospel to Jews from all over the world, the Lord gave them the "green light" by baptizing them with the Holy Spirit, providing them the ability to deliver the gospel in every language.

> *And they were all filled with the Holy Spirit and began to speak with other tongues, as the Spirit was giving them utterance. Now there were Jews living in Jerusalem, devout men from every nation under heaven. And when this sound occurred, the crowd came together, and were bewildered because each one of them was hearing them speak in his own language. They were amazed and astonished, saying, "Why, are not all these who are speaking Galileans? And how is it that we each hear them in our own language to which we were born? Parthians and Medes and Elamites, and residents of Mesopotamia, Judea and Cappadocia, Pontus and Asia, Phrygia and Pamphylia, Egypt and the districts of Libya around Cyrene, and visitors from Rome, both Jews and proselytes, Cretans and Arabs—we hear them in our own tongues speaking of the mighty deeds of God." And they all continued in amazement and great perplexity, saying to one another, "What does this mean?"*
>   *Acts 2:4–12*

From this chapter onward, the apostles continue to carry the gospel to the Jews as Jesus ordered in Acts 1:8—"in Jerusalem, and in all Judea and Samaria…"

For a decade or so, the gospel was delivered to their kinsmen only. When it was time to take the gospel to Gentiles—the remotest part of the earth—those Paul refers to as "far off" in Ephesians 2:13, God gave the "green light" again. This signal was obviously needed. Peter was initially resistant to the idea of taking the gospel to the Gentiles (as shown in Acts 10), and once Peter did take the gospel to them, the Jewish Christians were hesitant to accept the Gentiles into fellowship (Acts 11). But when the Gentiles in Cornelius' household received the baptism with the Holy Spirit, Peter asked:

> *Surely no one can refuse the water for these to be baptized who have received the Holy Spirit just as we did, can he?*
> *Acts 10:47*
>
> *"And I remembered the word of the Lord, how He used to say, 'John baptized with water, but you will be baptized with the Holy Spirit.' Therefore if God gave to them the same gift as He gave to us also after believing in the Lord Jesus Christ, who was I that I could stand in God's way?" When they heard this, they quieted down and glorified God, saying, "Well then, God has granted to the Gentiles also the repentance that leads to life."*
> *Acts 11:16–18*

The purposes of the baptism with the Holy Spirit were:

1. To provide confirming miraculous powers to the recipients.
2. To show that God expected His messengers to deliver the gospel to a new people group.

IS THE BAPTISM WITH THE HOLY SPIRIT FOR TODAY?

Jesus was always the administrator of the baptism with the Holy Spirit. We should not—cannot—administer, command, or pray for this baptism today, as disciples in the Scriptures never did. In fact, in the two explicit instances of the baptism with the Holy Spirit, it was a sudden event orchestrated completely by the will of God. There was no prayer by the recipients for the Holy Spirit to "come." There was no commandment for the recipients to "receive the Spirit." In the first case, Jesus told the apostles, "you will be baptized with the Holy Spirit not many days from now" (Acts 1:5). But when it did happen, the text still describes it as a *sudden* event.

> *And **suddenly** there came from heaven a noise like a violent rushing wind, and it filled the whole house where they were sitting.*
> *Acts 2:2*

When the Gentiles received the baptism with the Holy Spirit, the text says:

> *While Peter was still speaking these words, the Holy Spirit*
> *fell upon all those who were listening to the message. All*
> *the circumcised believers who came with Peter were*
> *amazed, because the gift of the Holy Spirit had been poured*
> *out on the Gentiles also.*
>
> *Acts 10:44–45*

The Gentile audience was understanding the message, but they had not yet responded to it. Before they did, the Lord poured His Spirit upon these people to communicate a message to the Jews.

Though the baptism with the Holy Spirit was an event we should thank God for, it was for specific purposes, which have already been fulfilled. There are other ways the Lord has provided His Holy Spirit. For instance, the Holy Spirit is provided to believers "as a pledge of our inheritance" (Ephesians 1:14). But a baptism with, the pouring out of, or immersion in the Holy Spirit or His power is not for today.

The gospels and epistles of the New Testament record several different types of baptisms.

- Water baptism administered by John the Baptist, and later by Jesus' disciples (Matthew 3:5–6; John 4:1–2)
- The baptism Jesus received, which took place at the same time as the previous baptism (Matthew 3:13–17)[7]
- Baptism with fire (Matthew 3:11)[8]

---

[7] Though Jesus was baptized by John in the wilderness, He received a different baptism than the rest of Judea. "John the Baptist appeared in the wilderness preaching a baptism of repentance for the forgiveness of sins. And all the country of Judea was going out to him…" (Mark 1:4–5). Jesus had no sins to be remitted (see Hebrews 4:14–16). Instead, He was baptized "to fulfill all righteousness" (Matthew 3:15).

[8] Many have assumed that baptism with fire is the same thing as baptism with the Holy Spirit, since they were both predicted at the same time. However, John explains in the next verse what baptism with fire will be like, which clearly links it with judgment of the unrighteous: "His winnowing fork is in His hand, and He will thoroughly clear His threshing floor; and He will gather His wheat into the barn, but He will burn up the chaff with unquenchable fire" (Matthew 3:12).

- Baptism of suffering (Mark 10:38)
- Baptism with the Holy Spirit (Acts 1:4–5)
- Baptism of Moses (1 Corinthians 10:2)
- Water baptism commanded of all nations (Matthew 28:19–20)

The letter to the Ephesians was written in about AD 62, which was 30 years after the first, and 20 years after the second recorded baptism with the Holy Spirit (Acts 2 and 10, respectively). Once the baptism with the Holy Spirit had been fulfilled, the apostle Paul wrote there is now only one baptism.

> *There is one body and one Spirit, just as also you were called in one hope of your calling; one Lord, one faith, **one baptism**, one God and Father of all who is over all and through all and in all.*
>
> *Ephesians 4:4–6*

Compare this passage with Acts 19:1–5, where Paul was in Ephesus, and he met men who had submitted to John's baptism after a different baptism—the *one* baptism—was in force.

> *When they heard this, they were baptized in the name of the Lord Jesus.*
>
> *Acts 19:5*

There is only one baptism commanded of all nations, which is not baptism with the Holy Spirit. When these men in Ephesus (the same place to which Paul wrote, "there is…one baptism") learned the truth, they rejected their previous understanding and submitted to God's commandment. They were not commanded to be baptized with the Holy Spirit. They were commanded to be baptized in the name of Jesus Christ. Therefore, if *we* have submitted to a different baptism, regardless of how sincere we were at the time, we must do the same. Reject the teachings of men, and embrace the commandments of God.

> *And Jesus came up and spoke to them, saying, "All authority has been given to Me in heaven and on earth. Go therefore and make disciples of all the nations, baptizing them in the name of the Father and the Son and the Holy Spirit, teaching them to observe all that I commanded you; and*

> *lo, I am with you always, even to the end of the age."*
> *Matthew 28:18–20*

Among the different baptisms mentioned in the New Testament, this baptism in Matthew 28—the only one ever commanded of the audience of the gospel—is what we see throughout the book of Acts and the epistles: baptism in water in the name of the Father, the Son, and the Holy Spirit. According to Jesus, this baptism is to be provided until the end of the age. All other baptisms were mentioned or promised, and they had their purposes in history, but only one baptism is commanded and unites someone with the death, burial, and resurrection of Jesus: baptism in water into Christ.

> *Or do you not know that all of us who have been baptized into Christ Jesus have been baptized into His death? Therefore we have been buried with Him through baptism into death, so that as Christ was raised from the dead through the glory of the Father, so we too might walk in newness of life. For if we have become united with Him in the likeness of His death, certainly we shall also be in the likeness of His resurrection, knowing this, that our old self was crucified with Him, in order that our body of sin might be done away with, so that we would no longer be slaves to sin; for he who has died is freed from sin.*
> *Romans 6:3–7*

This is the same baptism that Peter commanded even those who were baptized with the Holy Spirit to submit to.

> *"Surely no one can refuse the water for these to be baptized who have received the Holy Spirit just as we did, can he?" And he ordered them to be baptized in the name of Jesus Christ. Then they asked him to stay on for a few days.*
> *Acts 10:47–48*[9]

---

[9] Some have denied what the Scriptures say regarding water baptism, because, as they reason, Cornelius received the Holy Spirit before he was baptized in water. However, Cornelius was not receiving the pledge of inheritance when he was baptized with the Holy Spirit. The pledge is a promise to believers (more on that in a future chapter), yet baptism with the Holy Spirit was given to these Gentiles before they had responded to the message of Jesus.

Baptism with the Holy Spirit was something the Lord did in the past. There is no scriptural reason for us to expect it today, because:

- It was never commanded. Instead, the Lord provided it suddenly to specific people for specific purposes.
- Only two events in the New Testament were explicitly called baptism with the Holy Spirit.
- It has fulfilled its purposes.
- There is only one baptism today.

However, we must not feel like we are missing out on anything. As we will study later in this book, the Holy Spirit certainly is a part of any true disciple's life, and the Holy Spirit looked forward to the day when the church would mature enough that the miraculous powers He provided were no longer needed. In God's eyes, we are in a better position to understand the Holy Spirit than the first-century Christians who were equipped with His miraculous power.

> *However, you are not in the flesh but in the Spirit, if indeed the Spirit of God dwells in you. But if anyone does not have the Spirit of Christ, he does not belong to Him. If Christ is in you, though the body is dead because of sin, yet the spirit is alive because of righteousness. But if the Spirit of Him who raised Jesus from the dead dwells in you, He who raised Christ Jesus from the dead will also give life to your mortal bodies through His Spirit who dwells in you.*
>
> *Romans 8:9–11*

DISCUSSION QUESTIONS

1. What was baptism with the Holy Spirit?

2. How many times was baptism with the Holy Spirit recorded in Scripture? Who received it?

3. Who administered it?

4. What were the purposes of baptism with the Holy Spirit?

5. Should we pray for baptism with the Holy Spirit today?

6. What stood out to you as particularly interesting or helpful in this chapter?

7. How does this study help you approach God with greater reverence?

DEEPER DEVOTION
www.cloudedbyemotion.com

6

HOW DID PEOPLE
RECEIVE MIRACULOUS GIFTS?

Many theologians have offered different descriptions of the current era in which we live under God's rule (i.e. dispensation; the religious system today). The Scriptures offer this title: "the last days."[1]

> *God, after He spoke long ago to the fathers in the prophets in many portions and in many ways, **in these last days** has spoken to us in His Son, whom He appointed heir of all things, through whom also He made the world.*
>
> *Hebrews 1:1–2*

Living in the last days is in contrast with living under Moses' Law, which was in effect before Jesus' death, and which has been fulfilled in Christ.[2] In fact, living in the last days is in contrast to any era prior to the crucifixion of Jesus Christ. Our task in this chapter is to see how people in the New Testament received miraculous gifts from Acts 1 onwards.

One way people received miraculous gifts after Jesus' resurrection was through the baptism with the Holy Spirit. After the apostles in Acts 2 and the Gentiles in Acts 10 were baptized with the Holy Spirit, they were able to miraculously speak in tongues. When someone was baptized with the Holy Spirit, that person

---

[1] When Old Testament prophets spoke of "the last days," they usually were speaking of specific events in the first century—particularly, the destruction of Jerusalem, which occurred in AD 70 (see Isaiah 2:1–4 and Micah 3:12–4:4). In that sense, "the last days" have already ended, seeing as the prophecies have been fulfilled, and life in Judaism as it was before Jerusalem's destruction is impossible today.

[2] See Hebrews 8:6–13 and 9:15–17.

was granted certain miraculous gifts from the Holy Spirit.

After Cornelius' household was baptized with the Holy Spirit, they were commanded to be baptized in water, which again shows water baptism and baptism with the Holy Spirit were two separate baptisms, and they provided different blessings.

> *For they were hearing them speaking with tongues and exalting God. Then Peter answered, "Surely no one can refuse the water for these to be baptized who have received the Holy Spirit just as we did, can he?" And he ordered them to be baptized in the name of Jesus Christ. Then they asked him to stay on for a few days.*
>
> Acts 10:46-48

Though some teach being baptized "in the name of the Father and the Son and the Holy Spirit" (Matthew 28:19) is different than being baptized "in the name of Jesus Christ" (Acts 2:38), the Scriptures see no difference. Jesus taught the apostles to baptize all nations "in the name of the Father and the Son and the Holy Spirit." A few days later, the apostles began to command people to be baptized "in the name of Jesus Christ." "In the name of" means "by the authority of" (such as "Stop, in the name of the law!").[3] If it is by the authority of Jesus, then by extension, it is also by the authority of the Father and the Holy Spirit.[4]

To be baptized "in the name of Jesus Christ" or "in the name of the Lord Jesus" (Acts 19:5) requires being baptized in water. In the above passage, Peter asked who could refuse *water* for these people to be baptized, and then he commanded the people to be baptized "in the name of Jesus Christ."

The baptism Jesus desires for all nations—in water for the forgiveness of sins—is the "one baptism" that is commanded today (Ephesians 4:5). It is the baptism we continually read about in the book of Acts and within the epistles of the New Testament.

---

[3] Compare with Acts 4:7.
[4] See John 12:49-50 and 16:12-15.

God accepts only one baptism today, and we know to only seek the blessings from the commandment to be baptized in the name of Jesus in water. Those blessings are having sins washed away (Acts 22:16), newness of life (Romans 6:3–4), the indwelling of the Holy Spirit (Romans 8:9–11), salvation (1 Peter 3:21), and a new family in the body of Christ (1 Corinthians 12:12–13).

All people, including you and me, are commanded to be baptized into Christ, but Jesus baptized only a few people with the Holy Spirit. After they received the baptism with the Holy Spirit, those people could perform certain miracles.

There is one other way that people received miraculous gifts after the resurrection of Jesus. That is by the laying on of the apostles' hands.

> *Now at this time while the disciples were increasing in number, a complaint arose on the part of the Hellenistic Jews against the native Hebrews, because their widows were being overlooked in the daily serving of food. So the twelve summoned the congregation of the disciples and said, "It is not desirable for us to neglect the word of God in order to serve tables. Therefore, brethren, select from among you seven men of good reputation, full of the Spirit and of wisdom, whom we may put in charge of this task. But we will devote ourselves to prayer and to the ministry of the word." The statement found approval with the whole congregation; and they chose Stephen, a man full of faith and of the Holy Spirit, and Philip, Prochorus, Nicanor, Timon, Parmenas and Nicolas, a proselyte from Antioch. And these they brought before the apostles; and after praying, they laid their hands on them. The word of God kept on spreading; and the number of the disciples continued to increase greatly in Jerusalem, and a great many of the priests were becoming obedient to the faith. And Stephen, full of grace and power, was performing great wonders and signs among the people.*
>
> Acts 6:1–8

Stephen is the first person recorded in the last days to have performed miracles other than the apostles.[5] Philip (not the apostle, but the one chosen with Stephen in Acts 6) is the second person, and we see him performing signs in Acts 8. How is it these men, and presumably the other five men chosen, were now able to perform miracles when no one other than the apostles were recorded as having this ability prior? The apostles laid their hands on them.[6]

Toward the beginning of Acts 8 Philip was in Samaria, preaching the gospel, while the Holy Spirit confirmed his message with signs. People, including Simon, a well-known magician of sorts, believed and were baptized.

> *But when they believed Philip preaching the good news about the kingdom of God and the name of Jesus Christ, they were being baptized, men and women alike. Even Simon himself believed; and after being baptized, he continued on with Philip, and as he observed signs and great miracles taking place, he was constantly amazed. Now when the apostles in Jerusalem heard that Samaria had received the word of God, they sent them Peter and John, who came down and prayed for them that they might receive the Holy Spirit. For He had not yet fallen upon any of them; they had simply been baptized in the name of the Lord Jesus.* **Then they began laying their hands on them, and they were receiving the Holy Spirit.** *Now when Simon saw that the Spirit was bestowed through the laying on of the apostles' hands, he offered them money, saying, "Give this authority to me as well, so that everyone on whom I lay my hands may receive the Holy Spirit." But Peter said to him, "May your silver perish with you, because you thought you*

---

[5] See Acts 2:43 and 5:12.

[6] These men were "full of the Spirit" (v. 3). As we will study later, the phrases, "full of the Holy Spirit" and "filled with the Spirit" in the book of Acts are almost always, if not always, descriptions of those with miraculous abilities. Therefore, Stephen and Philip may have already been able to perform miracles prior to this moment. If so, the laying on of hands in this passage would have been for the purpose of sending them out to this ministry (cf. Acts 13:3). If these seven men could perform miracles prior to the events of Acts 6, the Scriptures still imply that it would have been by the laying on of the apostles' hands.

could obtain the gift of God with money! You have no part or portion in this matter, for your heart is not right before God. Therefore repent of this wickedness of yours, and pray the Lord that, if possible, the intention of your heart may be forgiven you. For I see that you are in the gall of bitterness and in the bondage of iniquity." But Simon answered and said, "Pray to the Lord for me yourselves, so that nothing of what you have said may come upon me."

Acts 8:12–24

These people had been baptized in the name of the Father, the Son, and the Holy Spirit. They were blessed with the promise of Ephesians 1:13–14:

In Him, you also, after listening to the message of truth, the gospel of your salvation—having also believed, you were sealed in Him with the Holy Spirit of promise, who is given as a pledge of our inheritance, with a view to the redemption of God's own possession, to the praise of His glory.

Though the Samaritan believers had the Holy Spirit of promise, there was clearly something from the Holy Spirit they did not have, which *only* the apostles were able to bestow through the laying on of their hands. Otherwise, Philip could have laid hands on them.

It happened that while Apollos was at Corinth, Paul passed through the upper country and came to Ephesus, and found some disciples. He said to them, "Did you receive the Holy Spirit when you believed?" And they said to him, "No, we have not even heard whether there is a Holy Spirit." And he said, "Into what then were you baptized?" And they said, "Into John's baptism." Paul said, "John baptized with the baptism of repentance, telling the people to believe in Him who was coming after him, that is, in Jesus." When they heard this, they were baptized in the name of the Lord Jesus. And when Paul had laid his hands upon them, the Holy Spirit came on them, and they began speaking with tongues and prophesying.

Acts 19:1–6

These men were baptized in water into Christ. Then, the apostle Paul laid his hands on them, and they were able to perform miracles.

Scripture records two ways people received miraculous gifts after the resurrection of Jesus:

1. Baptism with the Holy Spirit
2. Laying on of the apostles' hands

Baptism with the Holy Spirit was a blessing reserved for specific people for specific purposes in the first century. Those purposes have been fulfilled, and the baptism with the Holy Spirit is no longer needed nor provided.

Is it possible for the apostles to bestow miraculous gifts to believers today? To answer that question, we must first ask if there are apostles in the church today, which we will explore in the next chapter.

DISCUSSION QUESTIONS

1. What do the Scriptures mean when they speak of the last days?

2. What were the two ways people received miraculous gifts in the last days?

3. Beyond the apostles, who were the first two people recorded with the ability to perform signs, wonders, and miracles in the last days?

4. What stood out to you as particularly interesting or helpful in this chapter?

5. How does this study help you approach God with greater reverence?

7

CAN WE HAVE APOSTLES TODAY?

The role of an apostle in the church was a role God gave to equip and edify the church, bringing disciples to maturity.[1] The word *apostle* comes from the Greek word *apostolos* (ἀπόστολος), meaning "one who is sent."[2]

The first time the Twelve are referred to as apostles is in Matthew 10, which is when Jesus equipped them with miraculous gifts and sent them to preach the gospel of the kingdom to Israel. These were men Jesus hand-picked and chose for this work.

A few years later, one of the apostles named Judas betrayed Jesus, which led to Jesus' arrest and crucifixion. When worldly grief set in, instead of repenting, Judas committed suicide, dying in his sin.[3] After the resurrection, before ascending to the Father, Jesus gathered the remaining eleven to commission them to be His witnesses and make disciples of all nations. Not long afterward, they were assembled together, and, according to prophecy, it was time for them to appoint Judas' replacement. On that occasion, Peter said:

> *"For it is written in the book of Psalms, 'Let his homestead be made desolate, and let no one dwell in it'; and, 'Let another man take his office.' Therefore it is necessary that of the men who have accompanied us all the time that the*

---

[1] See Ephesians 4:11–12.

[2] In Acts 14:14, Barnabas, though not an official apostle of the Lord, is called an "apostle." This is because he was sent by the Holy Spirit on this journey in Acts 13:1–4. The same could be said of Epaphroditus (Philippians 2:25); Titus (2 Corinthians 8:23); and James, the brother of Jesus (Galatians 1:19). When we ask, "How did people become apostles?" in this book, we are interested in the official role of apostle, not the generic sense of one who was sent.

[3] See 2 Corinthians 7:9–10.

Lord Jesus went in and out among us—beginning with the baptism of John until the day that He was taken up from us—one of these must become a witness with us of His resurrection." So they put forward two men, Joseph called Barsabbas (who was also called Justus), and Matthias. And they prayed and said, "You, Lord, who know the hearts of all men, show which one of these two You have chosen to occupy this ministry and apostleship from which Judas turned aside to go to his own place." And they drew lots for them, and the lot fell to Matthias; and he was added to the eleven apostles.

Acts 1:20–26

Jesus was not on the earth to hand-pick Judas' replacement, so the apostles did it. But they knew whoever was chosen must meet certain criteria, as this man would be fulfilling what God originally assigned to Judas. The criteria put forward were:

1.   He had to be male (v. 21).
2.   He must have accompanied Jesus during His physical, earthly ministry (v. 21).
3.   He must have been an eyewitness of the resurrection (v. 22).

And even after one met all of those criteria,

4.   The new apostle still had to be chosen by the Lord Himself (vv. 24–26).[4]

This is the only case in the Scriptures where men were involved in any way in appointing someone to apostleship, though the Lord did the actual appointing. But Matthias was not the last apostle appointed in the New Testament. Later, we are introduced to Saul, a Pharisee bent on destroying God's church. In Acts 9, he was on his way to Damascus to persecute Christians, and Jesus appeared to him. Jesus' appearance convicted Saul of the truth, driving him to fast and pray for three days, an appropriate response.

This is a perfect example of how experiences and feelings are

---

[4] See also Proverbs 16:33.

untrustworthy sources of truth. Though he was sincere in living "with a perfectly good conscience before God" (Acts 23:1), Saul was sincerely wrong. Thank God he did not die in that state of rebellion, but he saw the error of his ways!

Later on, Saul, who also went by the name Paul, was known as an official apostle in the church. How did that happen? The Lord Himself chose him as He did the original Twelve and Matthias.

> *Paul, an apostle (**not sent from men nor through the agency of man, but through Jesus Christ and God the Father, who raised Him from the dead**), and all the brethren who are with me, to the churches of Galatia: Grace to you and peace from God our Father and the Lord Jesus Christ, who gave Himself for our sins so that He might rescue us from this present evil age, according to the will of our God and Father, to whom be the glory forevermore. Amen.*
>
> Galatians 1:1–5

How did people receive apostleship in the church? Jesus hand-picked them while He was on the earth. When men got involved, the prospective apostle must have met certain qualifications, as seen above. Who on earth today walked with Jesus before His death? No one. Who on earth today walked with Jesus after His resurrection? No one. Therefore, no one meets the qualifications for us to appoint him to apostleship today, and it would be sinful and utterly foolish to say to God, "Your requirements are not important to us. We will go ahead and appoint apostles anyway." But that is what so many in the religious world are trying to do. From Roman Catholicism to Protestantism to Mormonism, there are many churches that are claiming to have apostolic succession today. But such claims go against what the Holy Spirit has revealed in His Scriptures.

False apostleship is not new. In fact, there were even people in New Testament times who pretended to be apostles, as Paul had to deal with in his letters to the Corinthians.

> *But what I am doing I will continue to do, so that I may cut off opportunity from those who desire an opportunity*

> to be regarded just as we are in the matter about which
> they are boasting. For such men are false apostles, deceitful
> workers, disguising themselves as apostles of Christ. No
> wonder, for even Satan disguises himself as an angel of
> light. Therefore it is not surprising if his servants also dis-
> guise themselves as servants of righteousness, whose end
> will be according to their deeds.
>
> *2 Corinthians 11:12–15*

As sincere as they may seem or even believe themselves to be, when men or women claim to be apostles today, they are deceitful workers, servants of Satan. That is not my judgment. Since no one on earth today can meet the qualifications of an apostle given in the Scriptures, God judges them.

For those who claim to be apostles today, give them the Scriptures' test. To prove his apostleship, Paul reminded the Corinthian Christians:

> *The signs of a true apostle were performed among you with
> all perseverance, by signs and wonders and miracles.*
>
> *2 Corinthians 12:12*

What are the signs, wonders, and miracles of a true apostle? Here are some of them:

- The miraculous ability to speak in coherent languages (Acts 2:4–11)
- Healing various diseases, including paralysis, on the spot with immediate, undeniable results (Acts 3:6–10; 5:15; 9:33–34; 14:8–10; 28:8–9)
- Raising the dead (Acts 9:40; 20:9–10)
- Striking men blind (Acts 13:9–12)
- Exorcising spirits (Acts 16:18)
- Surviving deadly snakebites (Acts 28:3–6)

The Holy Spirit says if a person is a true apostle, then God has equipped him with these gifts. Can anyone today pass the test? Heal paralysis? Raise the dead? No. We are not talking about modern-day so-called "faith healers" who supposedly help with back pain. Again, compare what some churches claim happens in their assemblies today with what happened in the New

Testament. Such claims are an insult to the work of the Holy Spirit. All of the apostles have died on earth, having gone to paradise without appointing successors. The first example of this is in Acts 12:2, where the apostle James was "put to death with a sword." From this point forward, the number of apostles was only decreasing. The writings of the New Testament cover about fifty years after this event, and no successor of James was ever appointed. We have no apostles of the church on earth today. Therefore, no one can receive miraculous gifts through the laying on of the apostles' hands today.

Considering that, plus the fact that baptism with the Holy Spirit was also restricted to the first century, we can conclude miraculous gifts are not for the church today. We are living in the age the Holy Spirit was looking forward to. To bring the church to maturity is what He provided the miraculous gifts for in the first place.

> Love never fails; but if there are gifts of prophecy, they will be done away; if there are tongues, they will cease; if there is knowledge, it will be done away. For we know in part and we prophesy in part; but when the perfect comes, the partial will be done away. When I was a child, I used to speak like a child, think like a child, reason like a child; when I became a man, I did away with childish things. For now we see in a mirror dimly, but then face to face; now I know in part, but then I will know fully just as I also have been fully known.
>
> 1 Corinthians 13:8–12
>
> And He gave some as apostles, and some as prophets, and some as evangelists, and some as pastors and teachers, for the equipping of the saints for the work of service, to the building up of the body of Christ; until we all attain to the unity of the faith, and of the knowledge of the Son of God, to a mature man, to the measure of the stature which belongs to the fullness of Christ.
>
> Ephesians 4:11–13

It was important for people living in the first century to

perform miracles of the Holy Spirit. Doing so confirmed the message of Jesus. After all, it was imperative—and still is—that the audience believed the message.[5] However, Jesus was not on earth anymore when the apostles preached and wrote about the gospel. Anyone could claim to be the Christ or that their friend was the Christ, risen from the dead and ascended to heaven. What could help people distinguish the true message from false messages?

> *For this reason we must pay much closer attention to what we have heard, so that we do not drift away from it. For if the word spoken through angels proved unalterable, and every transgression and disobedience received a just penalty, how will we escape if we neglect so great a salvation? After it was at the first spoken through the Lord, it was confirmed to us by those who heard, God also testifying with them, both by signs and wonders and by various miracles and by gifts of the Holy Spirit according to His own will.*
>
> *Hebrews 2:1–4*

The apostles and the Holy Spirit went forth from Jesus' presence as witnesses to the truthfulness of His gospel. They performed signs only God could perform. They did so to prove to their audiences Jesus was the Christ, the Son of God. He has defeated death by rising from the dead, and He has now ascended to heaven and is reigning at the right hand of God.

> *Therefore many other signs Jesus also performed in the presence of the disciples, which are not written in this book; but these have been written so that you may believe that Jesus is the Christ, the Son of God; and that believing you may have life in His name.*
>
> *John 20:30–31*

God has gone to miraculous measures for us to have access to the words of life, which are "everything pertaining to life and godliness" (2 Peter 1:3), that we may be "equipped for every good work" (2 Timothy 3:17).

---

[5] See John 8:24.

When God's word is available, miracles are neither needed nor provided. Are we still craving signs? Would Jesus say of us, "An evil and adulterous generation craves for a sign" (Matthew 12:39)? Is our faith so weak it must be propped up with sight? No, we must have the faith the Holy Spirit seeks to impart within us.

> *Therefore, being always of good courage, and knowing that while we are at home in the body we are absent from the Lord— for we walk by faith, not by sight.*
>
> *2 Corinthians 5:6–7*
>
> *Now faith is the assurance of things hoped for, the conviction of things not seen.*
>
> *Hebrews 11:1*
>
> *So faith comes from hearing, and hearing by the word of Christ.*
>
> *Romans 10:17*

People are not performing miraculous gifts of the Holy Spirit today. Despite what the Scriptures say, there still are some who believe in miraculous works of the Holy Spirit among churches in the twenty-first century, most commonly claiming they can speak in tongues. In the next chapter, we will learn from every passage of Scripture that mentions the gift of tongues.

DISCUSSION QUESTIONS

1. How did the original twelve become apostles?

2. What were the qualifications of an apostle when men were involved in appointing someone to apostleship?

3. What were some of the signs of a true apostle of Jesus Christ?

4. Can we have apostles today? How do you know?

5. What does that mean regarding the ability to pass on miraculous gifts?

6. What stood out to you as particularly interesting or helpful in this chapter?

7. How does this study help you approach God with greater reverence?

 *DEEPER DEVOTION* *www.cloudedbyemotion.com*

8

WHAT WAS THE GIFT OF TONGUES?

The music slowed and became hushed and slightly hypnotic. The pastor said a monotone prayer, inviting the Spirit to make His presence known. "Thank you, Jesus!" the pastor said. "She's been slain in the Spirit!"

I craned my neck to see the person the preacher was indicating. A moment later, a lady emerged from the crowd, her arms spread out, eyes closed. "Totahshahee misa venday kontres trovusey todo shupé konda podakayeet-eh contrait…"

My friend, Mick, nudged me. "You see, bro. Anyone can speak in tongues. You have to open yourself up to the Spirit."

Not me, I thought. I had tried and failed.

I admit the first few times I visited an Apostolic Church in the summer of 2003, I was a bit scared by what I witnessed: people running around with outbursts of "Hallelujah!" "Praise the Lord!" "Thank you, Jesus!" and many things that definitely were not English. What I heard was unintelligible speech. What they claimed was, though they had no idea what they were saying, they were speaking to God in uncontrollable, "unknown tongues" and "tongues of angels."

Though outsiders called it gibberish, I had many reasons to trust these people. They were sincere. They were my friends. They had my best interests in mind. When I inquired more about this supposed "gift of tongues," they told me I had to be dunked in water (they called it baptism), and afterward I, too, could speak in tongues. That was apparently important, because they claimed speaking in tongues is the way God always shows believers they are saved. Of course, that was appealing.

A few days later, I allowed their leader to dunk me in water in a feeding trough. Coming out of the water, the audience waited. I waited. How did it work? Did God simply take over your tongue? Did you have to start speaking, and then it happened? I didn't know, so I tried everything. But nothing beyond my control occurred.

When I was unable to do what they did, which we thought was speaking in tongues, we were a bit concerned. I was told I needed to have more faith; however, that was the moment in life I was sure I had the most faith possible. Apparently, it wasn't enough.

Another friend who was not part of the Apostolic Church did something for me that surprised me. He gently asked, "What does the Bible say about tongues?" I had no idea. I assumed my friends knew, but they never showed it to me in the Scriptures, or even referenced the Scriptures, when talking about tongues. This led me on a journey to seek the truth for myself.[1]

* * * * * * *

The three questions I would like to focus on in this chapter are the same questions I had many years ago. According to the Scriptures,

1. What is the gift of tongues?
2. What was the purpose of the gift of tongues?
3. What about modern religious groups who allegedly practice the gift of tongues today?

As much as my religious friends talked about the spiritual gift, I was surprised to learn only three books in the Bible explicitly mention the gift of tongues. I'm pretty certain that what they thought was the gift of tongues was an extremely significant part of their belief system. However, in the scheme of things, the gift of tongues is a simple and small subject in the Scriptures.

The exhaustive list of passages that give us information about the gift of tongues is:

*   Mark 16:15–20
*   Acts 2:1–12; 10:44–48; 19:1–7

---

[1] For the rest of this story, see my book, *Transformed: A Spiritual Journey.*

- Chapters 12–14 of 1 Corinthians

It will be our task to study these passages, and a few others, to answer our questions. However, if you were to put down this book and read those passages yourself, you would likely learn all you need to know.

WHAT IS THE GIFT OF TONGUES?

The first time anyone spoke in tongues was on the first Pentecost after the resurrection of Jesus.[2]

> *When the day of Pentecost had come, they were all together in one place. And suddenly there came from heaven a noise like a violent rushing wind, and it filled the whole house where they were sitting. And there appeared to them tongues as of fire distributing themselves, and they rested on each one of them. And they were all filled with the Holy Spirit and began to speak with other tongues, as the Spirit was giving them utterance. Now there were Jews living in Jerusalem, devout men from every nation under heaven. And when this sound occurred, the crowd came together, and were bewildered because each one of them was hearing them speak in his own language. They were amazed and astonished, saying, "Why, are not all these who are speaking Galileans? And how is it that we each hear them in our own language to which we were born? Parthians and Medes and Elamites, and residents of Mesopotamia, Judea and Cappadocia, Pontus and Asia, Phrygia and Pamphylia, Egypt and the districts of Libya around Cyrene, and visitors from Rome, both Jews and proselytes, Cretans and Arabs—we hear them in our own tongues speaking of the mighty deeds of God." And they all continued in amazement and great perplexity, saying to one another, "What does this mean?"*
>
> *Acts 2:1–12*

First, we will note the baptism with the Holy Spirit is one way

---

[2] This is one of the reasons why one of the largest denominations supposedly practicing this gift calls themselves "Pentecostals."

God gave the gift of tongues to believers—in this case, the apostles. The same thing happened to Gentiles about ten years later in Acts 10. As we already learned from the Scriptures, we do not have the baptism with the Holy Spirit today. The other way God gave the gift of tongues was through the laying on of an apostle's hands.

> *And when Paul had laid his hands upon them, the Holy Spirit came on them, and they began speaking with tongues and prophesying.*
>
> *Acts 19:6*

The laying on of the apostles' hands cannot occur today, as the apostles have all died, and they have no successors on earth.

More important to our question at hand, Acts 2:1–12 (quoted above) is the most helpful of all to understand what the gift of tongues was. Verse 4 says the Holy Spirit was giving them utterance through the gift of tongues. He was providing the gift of this miraculous speech.

> *And when this sound occurred, the crowd came together, and were bewildered because each one of them was hearing them speak in his own language.*
>
> *Acts 2:6*

To speak in tongues was to speak in languages—actual known and understandable languages. This is similar to when someone asks, "What is your mother tongue?" The person is asking, "What is your native language?"

In the next two verses the crowds noted that the apostles were uneducated, yet they were speaking in every dialect known from every nation under heaven. The apostles were boldly speaking of the works of God to people in different languages, having never studied those languages prior. This is what the crowds noticed:

- "each one of them was hearing them speak in his own language" (v. 6).
- "all these who are speaking [are] Galileans" (v. 7).
- "we each hear them in our own language [or dialect] to which we were born" (v. 8).

- "we hear them in our own tongues speaking of the mighty deeds of God" (v. 11).

Is there any doubt those speaking in tongues were speaking *real*, known languages (not unintelligible speech or gibberish)? Is there any doubt the audiences could understand the words spoken by the tongue-speakers? No. The gift of tongues was a miraculous gift that gave the speaker the ability to speak a language with clarity—a language which he had never learned before.

I have heard some people defend the idea of unintelligible speech by claiming they were speaking "the tongues of angels." Where does this idea come from? In a passage we will study in depth in the next chapter of this book, Paul makes the point that love is supreme, but tongues were temporary. And he hypothetically says:

> *If I speak with the tongues of men and of angels, but do not have love, I have become a noisy gong or a clanging cymbal.*
>
> *1 Corinthians 13:1*[3]

In a passage where the apostle says tongues will cease (v. 8), people pull out of it that we can speak the "tongues of angels" on earth today. However, it is clear to see Paul is actually using a hyperbole to emphasize the value of love, not for us to take an obscure phrase and turn it into a doctrine. Once again, the gift of tongues described in the Scriptures was the miraculous ability to speak known *human* languages.

WHY DID GOD GRANT THE GIFT OF TONGUES?

My friend, John, went to Taiwan to teach the gospel, but he had to spend his first year there naturally learning the Chinese language with classes, tutors, homework, and so on. Likewise, my friend, Mark, went to Slovakia to preach the gospel. Again, he had to spend time naturally learning a language. But with the

---

[3] The hyperbolic nature of this statement is made clear two verses later where Paul says, "if I surrender my body to be burned, but do not have love, it profits me nothing."

gift of tongues, no time or learning was needed. The Holy Spirit miraculously provided the teacher the immediate ability to teach the gospel in any language needed.

Consider the first time Jesus sent His apostles out on a mission.

> *Jesus summoned His twelve disciples and gave them authority over unclean spirits, to cast them out, and to heal every kind of disease and every kind of sickness. Now the names of the twelve apostles are these: The first, Simon, who is called Peter, and Andrew his brother; and James the son of Zebedee, and John his brother; Philip and Bartholomew; Thomas and Matthew the tax collector; James the son of Alphaeus, and Thaddaeus; Simon the Zealot, and Judas Iscariot, the one who betrayed Him. These twelve Jesus sent out after instructing them: "Do not go in the way of the Gentiles, and do not enter any city of the Samaritans; but rather go to the lost sheep of the house of Israel. And as you go, preach, saying, 'The kingdom of heaven is at hand.' Heal the sick, raise the dead, cleanse the lepers, cast out demons. Freely you received, freely give.*
>
> *Matthew 10:1–8*

Anyone could have claimed the kingdom was near and the King had arrived. But if the Scriptures had not yet been written to confirm those facts, how would the audience have known if a messenger was really speaking the truth? In the case of the apostles, who really were proclaiming the truth, God provided the speakers with miracles. Jesus told them, "Heal the sick, raise the dead, cleanse the lepers, cast out demons." Did you notice what gift was not provided on this occasion? Jesus did not give them the gift of tongues, because He was sending them to their kinsmen of the same region—the lost sheep of the house of Israel. While they went out into the streets of their own neighborhoods, they did not need a variety of languages to teach the gospel of the kingdom; therefore, the gift of tongues was neither needed nor provided.

Fast forward a few years. About forty days after His

resurrection, Jesus summoned the same men (minus Judas) to give them a similar commission. But this time, all the nations were to receive the news of the resurrection and the arrival of the kingdom.

> *And He said to them, "Go into all the world and preach the gospel to all creation. He who has believed and has been baptized shall be saved; but he who has disbelieved shall be condemned. These signs will accompany those who have believed: in My name they will cast out demons, they will speak with new tongues; they will pick up serpents, and if they drink any deadly poison, it will not hurt them; they will lay hands on the sick, and they will recover." So then, when the Lord Jesus had spoken to them, He was received up into heaven and sat down at the right hand of God. And they went out and preached everywhere, while the Lord worked with them, and confirmed the word by the signs that followed.*
>
> Mark 16:15–20

This passage, which is the first time in Scripture the gift of tongues is explicitly mentioned, parallels the passage where Jesus told the same apostles:

> *But you will receive power when the Holy Spirit has come upon you; and you shall be My witnesses both in Jerusalem, and in all Judea and Samaria, and even to the remotest part of the earth.*
>
> Acts 1:8

The apostles were not being sent only to their neighborhood this time. They were also being sent to "make disciples of all the nations" (Matthew 28:19). Again, there was no written and confirmed Scripture yet that taught sinners of the need to repent and be baptized in the name of Jesus Christ, yet it still needed to be proclaimed. To prove the message was true, God confirmed their message with the signs that followed. In addition to confirming their message, the gift of tongues also aided them in proclaiming to those of other nations who spoke different languages.

The reason why this topic is scary or mysterious to many who are religious is because they have not cracked the spine of a Bible to learn how the gift of tongues worked. Instead, they are clouded by emotion when they witness excited people in church buildings doing what they *think* is speaking in tongues. I mean no offense, but it should bother us to the core that sincere religious people are distorting what should be viewed as a beautiful gift that perfectly fit into the plans of God to announce salvation to the captive. Instead, it has turned into an emotionally driven experience that benefits only those of an exclusive club. But the "benefits" that people claim come from this supposed gift in modern churches are not benefits at all. Instead, they are adrenaline rushes, emotional highs, and exciting spectacles that block out the true gospel. And because tongues is often seen as a rite of passage in some churches today, many people have felt driven to fake the gift in order to feel accepted. I admit that it crossed my mind when I didn't receive the gift in the Apostolic Church.

WHAT ABOUT MODERN RELIGIOUS GROUPS WHO ALLEGEDLY PRACTICE THE GIFT OF TONGUES TODAY?

There are three common false teachings about tongues today that many people believe.

1. Some believe speaking unintelligible speech, something no one on earth can understand, is the manifestation of the gift of tongues.
2. Some believe every Christian is expected to, or at least has the opportunity to, speak in tongues.
3. Some believe tongues were meant to be a permanent miraculous gift in the church.

I have spent some careful time in Bible study with friends who have believed all three of these false teachings. When asked, they are unable to explain what happens to them inwardly when they do their "speaking in tongues." Though some false teachers have purposely deceived many on this subject, I do not believe every so-called tongue-speaker is faking it.

Simply because it seems unexplainable does not mean it is from God. Even after careful study, some of my friends have stared straight at the Scriptures and admitted what they experience in their gatherings is *not* biblical tongues. Yet they also say they love the sensation and feel it makes them more spiritual and connected with God. One friend admitted when he thinks he is speaking in tongues, he is "overcome with uncontrollable babble." Most of the people I personally know who do this think modern "tongue-speaking" is a vital aspect of their faith, their church life, and their devotion to God. The idea of removing or changing it would be unthinkable. To say they are sincere in this practice, albeit a practice God never authorizes, is an understatement. But they also fit the description of Paul's kinsmen.

> *For I testify about them that they have a zeal for God, but not in accordance with knowledge. For not knowing about God's righteousness and seeking to establish their own, they did not subject themselves to the righteousness of God.*
>
> *Romans 10:2–3*

I hurt for my friends who value their emotional experiences over the commandments and promises in Scripture. With no scriptural backing, I am left to wonder if there is a psychological, scientific explanation involving adrenaline or other biological chemicals that overcome their bodies. Or is this the spiritual work of Satan? God knows.

> *But now, brethren, if I come to you speaking in tongues, what will I profit you unless I speak to you either by way of revelation or of knowledge or of prophecy or of teaching? Yet even lifeless things, either flute or harp, in producing a sound, if they do not produce a distinction in the tones, how will it be known what is played on the flute or on the harp? For if the bugle produces an indistinct sound, who will prepare himself for battle? So also you, unless you utter by the tongue speech that is clear, how will it be known what is spoken? For you will be speaking into the air. There are, perhaps, a great many kinds of languages in the world, and no kind is without meaning. If then I do not know the meaning of the language, I will be to the one who speaks a*

> *barbarian, and the one who speaks will be a barbarian to me.*

> *1 Corinthians 14:6–11*

Apparently in the first-century church, some Christians were tempted to flaunt their spiritual gifts, particularly the gift of tongues. They thought being able to speak in many languages made them look and sound sophisticated. Paul wrote to them to show their error, and his description of their immaturity also describes well the modern-day practice of "speaking in tongues." Tongues were not meant to be spoken at every occasion, but only when they would edify the listener. If the audience could not understand what was being spoken, then the effort was more than meaningless; it was counter-productive.

When Paul said "barbarian," he was saying if I cannot understand what you're saying, or if no one interprets what you're saying, then you simply sound *foreign*. However, when we use that word today, we sometimes mean to say someone is out of their mind. I do not mean to be insensitive, but when outsiders look at what churches are doing today—succumbing to uncontrollable babble—they sometimes wonder why the God of the universe of all wisdom and order would bless His people with the ability to speak in what amounts to gibberish. I wonder that too.

> *On the contrary, it is much truer that the members of the body which seem to be weaker are necessary; and those members of the body which we deem less honorable, on these we bestow more abundant honor, and our less presentable members become much more presentable, whereas our more presentable members have no need of it. But God has so composed the body, giving more abundant honor to that member which lacked, so that there may be no division in the body, but that the members may have the same care for one another. And if one member suffers, all the members suffer with it; if one member is honored, all the members rejoice with it. Now you are Christ's body, and individually members of it. And God has appointed in the church, first apostles, second prophets, third teachers, then miracles, then gifts of healings, helps,*

administrations, various kinds of tongues.
1 Corinthians 12:22–28

When tongues were spoken in the early church, it was to be done in order. What I have witnessed in modern churches who flaunt this supposed gift is they all try to speak at once. And, as my friend admitted, they believe this to be an uncontrollable thing. They claim they are overcome by the Holy Spirit. However, God commanded tongue-speakers to be silent on occasions and to wait for each other. Clearly, speaking in tongues was controllable.[4] There was a time to utilize it. There was a time to stay silent.

I was told God provides all believers with the gift of tongues—this ability to speak in unintelligible speech—to prove their salvation. However, even when the true gift of tongues was being employed, not every believer had the gift.

> *But to each one is given the manifestation of the Spirit for the common good. For to one is given the word of wisdom through the Spirit, and to another the word of knowledge according to the same Spirit; to another faith by the same Spirit, and to another gifts of healing by the one Spirit, and to another the effecting of miracles, and to another prophecy, and to another the distinguishing of spirits, to another various kinds of tongues, and to another the interpretation of tongues. But one and the same Spirit works all these things, distributing to each one individually just as He wills.*
> *1 Corinthians 12:7–11*

Later Paul asks, "All do not speak with tongues, do they?" (v. 30). No, not everyone in the first-century church was given the gift of tongues. Paul later says Christians were not extra special, extra spiritual, or more accepted in God's eyes if they did speak in tongues. Paul does not tie the gift of tongues to the assurance of salvation. To the contrary, in the following verses, he points to their baptism as their assurance that they belong in the body

---

[4] Prophecy was also a controllable gift (see 1 Corinthians 14:31–32). In fact, all gifts of grace were and are (see 1 Corinthians 12 and Romans 12).

of Christ.

> *For even as the body is one and yet has many members, and all the members of the body, though they are many, are one body, so also is Christ. For by one Spirit we were all baptized into one body, whether Jews or Greeks, whether slaves or free, and we were all made to drink of one Spirit.*
>
> *1 Corinthians 12:12–13*

There was an expiration date on miraculous gifts in the church.

> *Love never fails; but if there are gifts of prophecy, they will be done away; if there are tongues, they will cease; if there is knowledge, it will be done away.*
>
> *1 Corinthians 13:8*

Faith, hope, and love would continue, but prophecy, tongues, and miraculous knowledge would cease. Jesus said:

> *Not everyone who says to Me, "Lord, Lord," will enter the kingdom of heaven, but he who does the will of My Father who is in heaven will enter. Many will say to Me on that day, "Lord, Lord, did we not prophesy in Your name, and in Your name cast out demons, and in Your name perform many miracles?" And then I will declare to them, "I never knew you; depart from Me, you who practice lawlessness."*
>
> *Matthew 7:21–23*

There were people then, and there are people now, who think they are approved of God because they're convinced they can do mighty works and miracles. But the question is, are they truly doing the will of the Father? Do they know Jesus?

There are only three books in the Bible that explicitly mention the gift of tongues, and we have looked at all three in this chapter. We have learned the gift of tongues was a masterful miracle of God to provide His messengers the power to teach the good news of Jesus, His name, and His kingdom to all nations, eliminating any language barriers. On the day of Pentecost after His resurrection, there was a beautiful combination of God's providence and miracles.

God's providence led thousands of people from all over the

world to a single city—the same city in which Jesus had instructed His apostles to begin preaching the gospel. God's miraculous works allowed these apostles to preach the gospel to the devout Jews who gathered. These people heard the gospel in not only their own languages, but also in their own dialects, carrying the nuances of words and meanings deep into their hearts.

> *Now when they heard this, they were pierced to the heart, and said to Peter and the rest of the apostles, "Brethren, what shall we do?"*
>
> *Acts 2:37*

God be praised for what He accomplished through His messengers by giving them the miraculous gift of tongues! Twelve men taught thousands. Three thousand obeyed. Those three thousand taught thousands more, and so on, until one day—and maybe that day is today—you were presented with the same information: Jesus of Nazareth died for your sins, He was buried, and He was raised on the third day to give you a hope of resurrection. "God has made Him both Lord and Christ—this Jesus whom you crucified" (Acts 2:36). He now reigns as King of kings, but also as the receiver of the humble.

Do not let false miracles distract you from the true gospel. The gift of tongues was a small and simple subject. God used that miracle to teach in the first century. Now, we have the Scriptures translated into hundreds of languages so you and I can receive the same commandment the crowds on the first Pentecost after Jesus' resurrection received:

> *Peter said to them, "Repent, and each of you be baptized in the name of Jesus Christ for the forgiveness of your sins; and you will receive the gift of the Holy Spirit. For the promise is for you and your children and for all who are far off, as many as the Lord our God will call to Himself."*
>
> *Acts 2:38–39*

DISCUSSION QUESTIONS

1. When Jesus sent out the apostles for the first time, did He grant them the gift of tongues? Why or why not?

2. What was the gift of tongues?

3. When Jesus sent out the apostles to all nations, did He grant them the gift of tongues? Why or why not?

4. Was the gift of tongues used in some cases to teach those who were not yet believers (see Acts 2 and 1 Corinthians 14:22)? If so, what does that imply about the gift and those who allegedly practice it today?

5. Did every believer in the first century have the gift of tongues?

6. What stood out to you as particularly interesting or helpful in this chapter?

7. How does this study help you approach God with greater reverence?

DEEPER DEVOTION
www.cloudedbyemotion.com

9

HOW WAS THE CHURCH
BROUGHT TO MATURITY?

Open the book of First Corinthians, and you will quickly realize that most of the Corinthian church's problems were caused by division. They divided over many things. Most notably, they divided over their teachers in the faith.

> *Now I mean this, that each one of you is saying, "I am of Paul," and "I of Apollos," and "I of Cephas," and "I of Christ." Has Christ been divided? Paul was not crucified for you, was he? Or were you baptized in the name of Paul?*
>
> *1 Corinthians 1:12–13*

Later in the letter, the apostle also deals with their division over spiritual gifts. He reminds them:

> *Now there are varieties of gifts, but the same Spirit. And there are varieties of ministries, and the same Lord. There are varieties of effects, but the same God who works all things in all persons. But to each one is given the manifestation of the Spirit for the common good.*
>
> *1 Corinthians 12:4–7*

Paul's message in this chapter was that even though God blessed them with different gifts, the blessings came through the one Spirit. Not only that, but the different gifts were also given so they could complement each other and work together as one body in Christ—just like each person's body is united as one, yet it is made up of different members.

> *So that there may be no division in the body, but that the members may have the same care for one another. And if one member suffers, all the members suffer with it; if one*

member is honored, all the members rejoice with it. Now
you are Christ's body, and individually members of it.

1 Corinthians 12:25–27

In chapter 12, the problem is explained. But in chapter 13, the core of the issue is dealt with. Though these Christians had miraculous gifts of the Holy Spirit, they were lacking something better, something more excellent.

But earnestly desire the greater gifts. And I show you a still more excellent way. If I speak with the tongues of men and of angels, but do not have love, I have become a noisy gong or a clanging cymbal. If I have the gift of prophecy, and know all mysteries and all knowledge; and if I have all faith, so as to remove mountains, but do not have love, I am nothing. And if I give all my possessions to feed the poor, and if I surrender my body to be burned, but do not have love, it profits me nothing. Love is patient, love is kind and is not jealous; love does not brag and is not arrogant, does not act unbecomingly; it does not seek its own, is not provoked, does not take into account a wrong suffered, does not rejoice in unrighteousness, but rejoices with the truth; bears all things, believes all things, hopes all things, endures all things. Love never fails; but if there are gifts of prophecy, they will be done away; if there are tongues, they will cease; if there is knowledge, it will be done away.

1 Corinthians 12:31–13:8

If only these Christians would have applied love to their gifts, they would not have been dividing. Tongues, prophecy, knowledge, faith, and works, all without love, are useless in the kingdom of God.

For we know in part and we prophesy in part; but when the perfect comes, the partial will be done away. When I was a child, I used to speak like a child, think like a child, reason like a child; when I became a man, I did away with childish things. For now we see in a mirror dimly, but then face to face; now I know in part, but then I will know fully just as I also have been fully known. But now faith, hope, love,

> *abide these three; but the greatest of these is love.*
>
> *1 Corinthians 13:9–13*

In 1 Corinthians 13, there are six things in focus: prophecy, tongues, knowledge, faith, hope, and love. Three of the six—prophecy, tongues, and knowledge—were temporary, and the other three—faith, hope, and love—were enduring.

First, we should note *knowledge* mentioned here is not standard knowledge, like two plus two equals four or Jesus died for our sins. It is that of supernatural, miraculous knowledge that was revealed by the Holy Spirit to the person having the gift of knowledge.

> *But to each one is given the manifestation of the Spirit for the common good. For to one is given the word of wisdom through the Spirit, and to another the word of knowledge according to the same Spirit.*
>
> *1 Corinthians 12:7–8*

> *But now, brethren, if I come to you speaking in tongues, what will I profit you unless I speak to you either by way of revelation or of knowledge or of prophecy or of teaching?*
>
> *1 Corinthians 14:6*

In the "bookends" to chapter 13, Paul talks about the miraculous gift of knowledge, which was used in conjunction with prophecy, tongues, revelation, and teaching. Remembering this was written in the first century, before the completed New Testament Scriptures were in the hands of believers, there were things Christians had to know, believe, and practice which they could not read about in what we know as the New Testament. Instead, the Holy Spirit provided that information through people He equipped with gifts like prophecy, tongues (that is, miraculously teaching without language barriers), and miraculous knowledge. But the Holy Spirit also said these spiritual gifts would eventually end.

> *Love never fails; but if there are gifts of prophecy, they will be done away; if there are tongues, they will cease; if there is knowledge, it will be done away. For we know in part and we prophesy in part; but when the perfect comes, the*

partial will be done away.
      1 Corinthians 13:8–10

Miraculous gifts would endure only until "the perfect" arrived. Beyond that, faith, hope, and love would abide.

```
prophecy ——— done away    ┊ when the perfect comes ┊
tongues ——————— cease      ┊                        ┊
knowledge ——— done away    ┊                        ┊
                           ┊                        ┊
                           ┊                        ┊
                           ┊                        ┊
                           ┊                        ┊
                           ┊                        ┊
                           ┊                        ┊
faith ————————— abides ———————————————————————————→
hope ————————— abides ————————————————————————————→
love ————————— never fails ———————————————————————→
```

Of course, this raises the question, what is "the perfect," and when did or when will it arrive? Right away, we can learn "the perfect" is not the second coming of Jesus, as some have suggested. The timeline is this: prophecy, tongues, knowledge, faith, hope, and love existed in the first century. At some point, spiritual gifts would end. Then, faith, hope, and love would remain *beyond* "the perfect."

Faith and hope will be fulfilled at the second coming of Jesus. Though we have never seen Jesus, the throne on which He reigns, or the works He will perform in the future, based on the confidence of the Scriptures, we do believe.

> *Now faith is the assurance of things hoped for, the conviction of **things not seen**.*
>   *Hebrews 11:1*

If faith is placed into that which is *unseen*, then the moment we *see* Jesus at His coming, such faith is no longer needed. It is fulfilled.

The same goes for hope. We hope for life in the eternal city of Jesus after the final resurrection. Again, when Jesus arrives and says, "Come, you who are blessed of My Father, inherit the kingdom prepared for you from the foundation of the world" (Matthew 25:34), then we no longer hope for that dwelling place.

> *And not only this, but also we ourselves, having the first fruits of the Spirit, even we ourselves groan within ourselves, waiting eagerly for our adoption as sons, the redemption of our body. For in hope we have been saved, but **hope that is seen is not hope; for who hopes for what he already sees?** But if we hope for what we do not see, with perseverance we wait eagerly for it.*
>
> *Romans 8:23–25*

At the coming of Jesus, when eternal life is fully granted, faith and hope will be satisfied and fulfilled.

> *For we walk by faith, not by sight.*
>
> *2 Corinthians 5:7*

However, love will never be obsolete. In John 17:24, Jesus says the Father loved Him before time began. The apostle John wrote in 1 John 4:7–13:

> *Beloved, let us love one another, for love is from God; and everyone who loves is born of God and knows God. The one who does not love does not know God, for God is love. By this the love of God was manifested in us, that God has sent His only begotten Son into the world so that we might live through Him. In this is love, not that we loved God, but that He loved us and sent His Son to be the propitiation for our sins. Beloved, if God so loved us, we also ought to love one another. No one has seen God at any time; if we love one another, God abides in us, and His love is perfected in us. By this we know that we abide in Him and He in us, because He has given us of His Spirit.*

God is love. God is eternal. Love is eternal, having neither beginning nor end. Although I do not expect time to be counted in eternity, a billion years from now, we will still love God. Of the six things in focus in 1 Corinthians 13, five of them—prophecy, tongues, knowledge, faith, and hope—are temporary. The Holy Spirit said spiritual gifts would cease when "the perfect" came. Faith and hope would last until the second coming of

Jesus. Beyond that, only love would continue. And that is why Paul says, "the greatest of these is love."

prophecy ——— done away
tongues ——————— cease
knowledge ——— done away

when the perfect comes

childhood | maturity
see dimly | see clearly
partial knowledge | complete knowledge

faith ———————— abides ————————————
hope ———————— abides ————————————
love ———————— never fails ————————————→

second coming of Jesus

eternity

[1]What can we learn about what this "perfect" item in question is? Our text tells us that before it came, the church was in its infancy, people saw dimly in a mirror, and they had access to partial knowledge. That means "that which is perfect," as the King James Version calls it, provides maturity, clear vision ("face-to-face"), and full knowledge.

This word *perfect* in this text comes from the Greek word *teleios* (τέλειος). Depending on the context, it can be translated as "mature," as it is in Hebrews 5:14, where the author speaks of Christians who grow in maturity and knowledge. Or it can mean "perfect" or "complete," meaning the state of wholeness as God sees it.[2]

What we will see from Scripture is "that which is perfect" in 1 Corinthians 13 is access to the completed word of God. Remember, at this point, the Christians only had access to the Old Testament Scriptures, and maybe a few of the New Testament writings.

Having limited access to God's will under the new covenant:

1. Provided only partial knowledge, allowing the average

---

[1] This graph was inspired by an illustration in Kevin L. Moore's *Personal Bible Study* series.
[2] See Matthew 5:48 and 19:21.

person only a dim view of God and His will.

2. Required miraculous gifts such as prophecy, tongues, and knowledge to convey what was lacking.

The completed word of God would provide maturity, clear vision through the revealed love of God, and complete knowledge of His revealed will. As the era of Holy Spirit inspiration was coming to a close, notice some of the things the apostles and prophets wrote.

> *And He gave some as apostles, and some as prophets, and some as evangelists, and some as pastors and teachers, for the equipping of the saints for the work of service, to the building up of the body of Christ;* **until we all attain to the unity of the faith, and of the knowledge of the Son of God, to a mature** [teleios] **man, to the measure of the stature which belongs to the fullness of Christ.** *As a result, we are no longer to be children, tossed here and there by waves and carried about by every wind of doctrine, by the trickery of men, by craftiness in deceitful scheming; but speaking the truth in love, we are to grow up in all aspects into Him who is the head, even Christ, from whom the whole body, being fitted and held together by what every joint supplies, according to the proper working of each individual part, causes the growth of the body for the building up of itself in love.*
>
> Ephesians 4:11–16

Certain gifts (like prophecy) were granted to the church for building up of maturity and knowledge. Paul knew the growth of the church was imminent, and soon, the Christians would grow to their full stature, having access to the entire doctrine of Christ.

> *Grace and peace be multiplied to you in the knowledge of God and of Jesus our Lord; seeing that His divine power has granted to us* **everything pertaining to life and godliness, through the true knowledge of Him** *who called us by His own glory and excellence. For by these He has granted to us His precious and magnificent promises, so that by*

> *them you may become partakers of the divine nature, having escaped the corruption that is in the world by lust.*
>
> *2 Peter 1:2–4*

Peter told the Christians they had access to everything needed for true knowledge and godliness.[3] To say someone has the gift of prophecy of the Holy Spirit today is to contradict God and say His will is still being revealed today, and we do not have what equips us for all good works. However, the faith has been "once for all handed down to the saints" (Jude 3). There is no wonder why the New Testament is full of warnings against false prophets. Peter would warn in the next chapter:

> *But false prophets also arose among the people, just as there will also be false teachers among you, who will secretly introduce destructive heresies, even denying the Master who bought them, bringing swift destruction upon themselves. Many will follow their sensuality, and because of them the way of the truth will be maligned; and in their greed they will exploit you with false words; their judgment from long ago is not idle, and their destruction is not asleep.*
>
> *2 Peter 2:1–3[4]*

> *And do not be conformed to this world, but be transformed by the renewing of your mind, so that you may prove what* **the will of God is, that which is good and acceptable and perfect** [teleios].
>
> *Romans 12:2*

Paul claims the will of God is *perfect*—the same word and phrase we see in 1 Corinthians 13:10.

> *I testify to everyone who hears the words of the prophecy of*

---

[3] At this point in time, the New Testament was not completed in written form, but these Christians did have everything they needed by way of oral and written teachings from the apostles and prophets. By the time 2 Peter was written, the letters of Paul were already circulating among Christians (see 2 Peter 3:14–18). Paul quoted from the gospel of Luke in 1 Timothy 5:18 (cf. Luke 10:7). Therefore, though not all of the New Testament was written and available, most of it seems to have been.

[4] See also Matthew 7:15–20; 1 John 4:1; and Revelation 16:13–14.

this book: if anyone adds to them, God will add to him the plagues which are written in this book; and if anyone takes away from the words of the book of this prophecy, God will take away his part from the tree of life and from the holy city, which are written in this book. He who testifies to these things says, "Yes, I am coming quickly." Amen. Come, Lord Jesus. The grace of the Lord Jesus be with all. Amen.

Revelation 22:18–21

The last warnings in Scripture are:

1. Do not add to Scripture.
2. Do not take away from Scripture.

These warnings originally applied to the book of Revelation, but I do not think it is an accident that this is also the last thing we read in the completed word of God. The last promise of Scripture pertains to Jesus' return. Scripture had been sealed. There would be no authorized additions to it. It would be sufficient for all knowledge and maturity until the day He comes to judge the world.

Paul claimed in the first century, "For now we see in a mirror dimly, but then [when "the perfect" comes] face to face" (1 Corinthians 13:12). Seeing "face to face" after "the perfect" comes is not a reference to seeing Jesus' face. It is a reference to being able to clearly see yourself the way God sees you through the mirror of the word of God. James calls the word "the perfect law, the law of liberty," which someone can look at as a mirror and see himself face-to-face. Are you simply hearing? Or are you also doing?

But prove yourselves doers of the word, and not merely hearers who delude themselves. For if anyone is a hearer of the word and not a doer, he is like a man who looks at his natural face in a mirror; for once he has looked at himself and gone away, he has immediately forgotten what kind of person he was. But one who looks intently at the perfect law, the law of liberty, and abides by it, not having become a forgetful hearer but an effectual doer, this man will be blessed in what he does.

James 1:22–25

As we have learned in previous studies, miraculous gifts were provided to confirm the word of God. The three miraculous gifts in view in 1 Corinthians 13—prophecy, tongues, and knowledge—specifically dealt with the communication of God's word. Those gifts would no longer be needed once the word of God had been completely written, confirmed, and preserved. Now that we have access to the word of God, miraculous gifts in the church are neither needed nor provided.

However, faith, hope, and love abide. Paul chastised the immaturity of Christians who desired the temporary things (miraculous gifts) over the enduring things. Would you rather be awestruck by fireworks and spiritual spectacles, or brought to your knees by the true knowledge of Jesus Christ? Do not allow false miracles in the twenty-first century to distract you from the true gospel of Jesus.

Do I believe in miracles? With all my heart. That is, true miracles. Do I believe in God's power today? Without a doubt. Do I believe the Scriptures? Every word. And those Scriptures tell me when "the perfect"—the completed word of God—came, miraculous gifts for Christians ceased and were done away with. What were they left with? Faith; hope; and the greatest gift of all, love.

> *If I speak with the tongues of men and of angels, but do not have love, I have become a noisy gong or a clanging cymbal. If I have the gift of prophecy, and know all mysteries and all knowledge; and if I have all faith, so as to remove mountains, but do not have love, I am nothing. And if I give all my possessions to feed the poor, and if I surrender my body to be burned, but do not have love, it profits me nothing. Love is patient, love is kind and is not jealous; love does not brag and is not arrogant, does not act unbecomingly; it does not seek its own, is not provoked, does not take into account a wrong suffered, does not rejoice in unrighteousness, but rejoices with the truth; bears all things, believes all things, hopes all things, endures all things.*

1 Corinthians 13:1–7

People have disagreed with what Scripture says on this subject because of what they have supposedly seen or experienced. But that is not new. Satan has used experience and emotion as weapons against righteousness from the beginning.

> *For such men are false apostles, deceitful workers, disguising themselves as apostles of Christ. No wonder, for even Satan disguises himself as an angel of light.*
>
> *2 Corinthians 11:13–14*

Jeremiah also warned the entire nation of Israel:

> *Blessed is the man who trusts in the LORD*
> *And whose trust is the LORD.*
> *For he will be like a tree planted by the water,*
> *That extends its roots by a stream*
> *And will not fear when the heat comes;*
> *But its leaves will be green,*
> *And it will not be anxious in a year of drought*
> *Nor cease to yield fruit.*
> **The heart is more deceitful than all else**
> **And is desperately sick;**
> **Who can understand it?**
> *I, the LORD, search the heart,*
> *I test the mind,*
> *Even to give to each man according to his ways,*
> *According to the results of his deeds.*
>
> *Jeremiah 17:7–10*

We have access to God's word today because of the miraculous measures of the Holy Spirit in the first century. Are you thankful for His word?

DISCUSSION QUESTIONS

1. What six things are in focus in 1 Corinthians 13?

2. Which were temporary? Which is permanent?

3. What kind of knowledge is this passage referencing?

4. What was Paul referring to when he wrote about the coming of "the perfect"?

5. Has "the perfect" come? If so, what does that mean?

6. What is "the perfect" able to accomplish within the disciple?

7. What stood out to you as particularly interesting or helpful in this chapter?

8. How does this study help you approach God with greater reverence?

*DEEPER
DEVOTION*
www.cloudedbyemotion.com

10
WHAT IS THE ETERNAL SIN?

I pulled into the driveway, willing my tires on the gravel to crunch quietly. I didn't want to wake my mom and step-dad. I walked up the back steps and slowly turned the key in the door. I silently made my way down the hallway, closed the door behind me, and turned on the light. First order of business: rid myself of the restaurant's grease-infested uniform.

Once changed, I did what had become my custom since August. I picked up my Bible and started reading. I had asked Devin, my closest Christian friend, where I should start for a good overview of the Bible, since I was a new Christian. He recommended I start with one of the gospel accounts. I opted for Mark, since it seemed to be the shortest one.

I turned to the bookmark, which had been placed at Mark 3. I read about how Jesus healed people. I read about when He chose the Twelve. Then, one of the scariest things in my life happened—I encountered Mark 3:28–29:

> *Truly I say to you, all sins shall be forgiven the sons of men, and whatever blasphemies they utter; but whoever blasphemes against the Holy Spirit never has forgiveness, but is guilty of an eternal sin.*

* * * * * * *

I suspect I am not the only one this passage has frightened. Questions flood the unsuspecting reader's mind. *What does it mean to blaspheme against the Holy Spirit? Have I committed that sin? If so, is it true I can never be forgiven? What will I receive on the day of judgment?*

In this chapter, we will address the following questions:

1. What does it mean to blaspheme the Holy Spirit?

2. Is it possible to blaspheme the Holy Spirit today?
3. What other ways can we sin against the Holy Spirit?

WHAT DOES IT MEAN TO BLASPHEME THE HOLY SPIRIT?

To blaspheme simply means to speak against. If Jesus could forgive those who blasphemed and even crucified Him,[1] then why can He not forgive someone who speaks against the Spirit, whether intentionally or carelessly? Is the value of the Spirit somehow greater than Jesus' value?

On the surface, this seems harsh and unreasonable. So long as we stay on the surface, we will continue with our questions unanswered, our accusations unfounded, and our fears unsettled. The first step to understanding a Scripture is to read it in its context. Even though the first time I read the passage, I read it in context, I did not pay attention. It scared me, so I isolated it and wondered how it applied to me directly. But the question I should have been asking is how did it apply to the first audience?

Jesus' popularity was growing due to His miracles and public teaching. The first miracle of Christ Mark records is the casting out an unclean spirit—a demon.

> *Just then there was a man in their synagogue with an unclean spirit; and he cried out, saying, "What business do we have with each other, Jesus of Nazareth? Have You come to destroy us? I know who You are—the Holy One of God!" And Jesus rebuked him, saying, "Be quiet, and come out of him!" Throwing him into convulsions, the unclean spirit cried out with a loud voice and came out of him. They were all amazed, so that they debated among themselves, saying, "What is this? A new teaching with authority! He commands even the unclean spirits, and they obey Him." Immediately the news about Him spread everywhere into all the surrounding district of Galilee.*
>
> *Mark 1:23–28*

---

[1] See Acts 2:36–38.

Mark also records in chapter 3 how the Pharisees, Herodians, and scribes were all conspiring to trap and destroy Him.

> *The scribes who came down from Jerusalem were saying, "He is possessed by Beelzebul," and "He casts out the demons by the ruler of the demons." And He called them to Himself and began speaking to them in parables, "How can Satan cast out Satan? If a kingdom is divided against itself, that kingdom cannot stand. If a house is divided against itself, that house will not be able to stand. If Satan has risen up against himself and is divided, he cannot stand, but he is finished! But no one can enter the strong man's house and plunder his property unless he first binds the strong man, and then he will plunder his house. Truly I say to you, all sins shall be forgiven the sons of men, and whatever blasphemies they utter; but whoever blasphemes against the Holy Spirit never has forgiveness, but is guilty of an eternal sin"— because they were saying, "He has an unclean spirit."*
>
> *Mark 3:22–30[2]*

Reading the greater context helps us understand this startling saying of Christ. Here is what happens in this passage:

1. The scribes say Jesus is possessed by and gains power from the ruler of the demons.
2. Jesus asks pointed questions to prove the absurdity of their accusations.
3. Jesus makes His statements about blasphemies and the eternal sin.
4. Mark, inspired by the Holy Spirit, gives Jesus' reason for saying this: "because they were saying, 'He has an unclean spirit'" (v. 30).

The "bookends" to this passage show us what Jesus was dealing with: a resistant force claiming He was filled with a demon and wielded Satan's power. In reality, Jesus was "full of the Holy Spirit" (Luke 4:1). When these people claimed Jesus was possessed by a demon, they were calling God's Holy Spirit an

---

[2] See also Matthew 12:22–45.

unclean spirit, even Satan himself. Among the list of unwise things to say, this must be near the top.

In other words, God was giving them conclusive proof that their Messiah was among them. That proof was the work of the Holy Spirit that Jesus demonstrated through miracles. They admitted that He truly was a miracle-worker. However, instead of accepting God's proof, they resorted to blaspheming the Holy Spirit, calling Him Satan. At that point, there was nothing else that would convince them. Their hearts were set on denying the one who came to save them. They had rejected their last chance for forgiveness.

As we have already studied, Jesus came with miracles to prove who He was, to testify of the gospel of the kingdom. Some saw the signs and believed.

> Now there was a man of the Pharisees, named Nicodemus, a ruler of the Jews; this man came to Jesus by night and said to Him, "Rabbi, we know that You have come from God as a teacher; for no one can do these signs that You do unless God is with him."
>
> John 3:1–2

Others, such as the scribes of Mark 3, saw the signs and blasphemed, and Jesus told these people that indirectly calling the Holy Spirit a demon was an eternal sin.

Those who truly believed Jesus was casting out demons by the ruler of the demons would never accept the testimony of the Holy Spirit. They would continue believing Jesus to be a messenger of Satan. Therefore, they would never go to the true source of forgiveness—Jesus Himself. Those who spoke against the Holy Spirit and His work would never accept the gospel in which there is "the power of God for salvation to everyone who believes" (Romans 1:16).

In a passage we will focus on more deeply in a later chapter, Jesus promised the apostles through their work, the Holy Spirit would "convict the world concerning sin and righteousness and judgment" (John 16:8). But when people reject and blaspheme the Holy Spirit, they will never come to a full conviction of sin, righteousness, and judgment. Without a serious understanding of sin and its consequences, how can repentance be realized?

The Holy Spirit was sent to be the final witness, alongside the apostles, to the fact Jesus is the Christ, the son of God.[3] These scribes had rejected the Father, and they were rejecting the Son. They were now blaspheming the last chance God was giving them. If they continued in that state, they would enter eternity without the Helper (the Holy Spirit), and without the Advocate (the Son of God), who was the propitiation for sins.[4]

IS IT POSSIBLE TO BLASPHEME THE HOLY SPIRIT TODAY?

Upon seeing the evidence the Holy Spirit has provided that Jesus is the Christ, the Son of the Living God, and ignoring, refusing, speaking against it—or worst of all, accepting it at first, but later denying it[5]—we too will face God's judgment. In that sense, yes, we can be condemned with these scribes.

> *For in the case of those who have once been enlightened and have tasted of the heavenly gift and have been made partakers of the Holy Spirit, and have tasted the good word of God and the powers of the age to come, and then have fallen away, it is impossible to renew them again to repentance, since they again crucify to themselves the Son of God and put Him to open shame.*
>
> *Hebrews 6:4–6*

Compare these two passages:

> *Truly I say to you, all sins shall be forgiven the sons of men, and whatever blasphemies they utter; but whoever blasphemes against the Holy Spirit never has forgiveness, but is guilty of an eternal sin"— because they were saying, "He has an unclean spirit."*
>
> *Mark 3:28–30*

---

[3] See John 15:26–27; 20:30–31; Acts 1:8; and 5:32.

[4] See John 16:7 and 1 John 2:1–2.

[5] See 2 Peter 2:20–22.

> *For if we go on sinning willfully **after receiving the knowledge of the truth, there no longer remains a sacrifice for sins**, but a terrifying expectation of judgment and the fury of a fire which will consume the adversaries. Anyone who has set aside the Law of Moses dies without mercy on the testimony of two or three witnesses. How much severer punishment do you think he will deserve who has trampled under foot the Son of God, and has regarded as unclean the blood of the covenant by which he was sanctified, and **has insulted the Spirit of grace**? For we know Him who said, "Vengeance is Mine, I will repay." And again, "The Lord will judge His people." It is a terrifying thing to fall into the hands of the living God.*
>
> Hebrews 10:26–31

These passages are not parallel passages, in that they refer to the same people. The latter passage was written to warn Christians (those who had already received God's forgiveness) of the dangers of leaving Christ, and thus, leaving salvation. However, the state of the heart of the two people is the same:

- He goes on sinning willfully after being exposed to the truth.
- He tramples the Son of God under foot.
- He regards the blood of the covenant as unclean.
- He insults the Spirit of grace.
- He will fall into the hands of the living God.

  > *And inasmuch as it is appointed for men to die once and after this comes judgment, so Christ also, having been offered once to bear the sins of many, will appear a second time for salvation without reference to sin, to those who eagerly await Him.*
  >
  > Hebrews 9:27–28

We are not in the same situation the scribes were in. In that sense, we cannot be guilty of the same sin. They saw Jesus in the flesh, whom the Holy Spirit had confirmed through His miracles—"Look! This is the Son of God whom you should serve with your life!" Yet, they were closed-minded and said the power within Jesus, which the Holy Spirit had provided, was the power of Satan.

We, on the other hand, are not witnessing first-hand the miracles worked by Jesus Himself. That does not mean, though, we are less accountable for our faith. We have the Scriptures, which the Holy Spirit has confirmed through His miracles—"Look! The living word of God, which will be the standard of eternal judgment! Be devoted to learning and obeying it, for it is My word!" Far be it from us to call the Scriptures "just a book," man-made, or one of many ways to know God's truth.

> *For this reason we must pay much closer attention to what we have heard, so that we do not drift away from it. For if the word spoken through angels proved unalterable, and every transgression and disobedience received a just penalty, how will we escape if we neglect so great a salvation? After it was at the first spoken through the Lord, it was confirmed to us by those who heard, God also testifying with them, both by signs and wonders and by various miracles and by gifts of the Holy Spirit according to His own will.*
> *Hebrews 2:1–4*

No, we cannot be guilty of the eternal sin the way the scribes were. But we are still expected to pay attention to and respond to what the Holy Spirit has accomplished. We must not neglect such a great salvation!

WHAT OTHER WAYS CAN WE SIN AGAINST THE HOLY SPIRIT?

One thing Jesus' warning regarding the eternal sin should do is cause us to evaluate carefully our reverence toward God. The apostles and prophets filled the New Testament with warnings that God takes our thoughts, words, and actions seriously. When we fill our hearts with lust, when we utter careless words, and when we tear down those created in His image, He takes those sins personally.

We can lie to the Holy Spirit

But a man named Ananias, with his wife Sapphira, sold a

> *piece of property, and kept back some of the price for himself, with his wife's full knowledge, and bringing a portion of it, he laid it at the apostles' feet. But Peter said, "Ananias, why has Satan filled your heart to lie to the Holy Spirit and to keep back some of the price of the land? While it remained unsold, did it not remain your own? And after it was sold, was it not under your control? Why is it that you have conceived this deed in your heart? You have not lied to men but to God."*
>
> Acts 5:1–4

When this couple attempted to deceive the body of Christ to gain the church's admiration, they lied to the Holy Spirit.

We can resist the Holy Spirit

> *You men who are stiff-necked and uncircumcised in heart and ears are always resisting the Holy Spirit; you are doing just as your fathers did. Which one of the prophets did your fathers not persecute? They killed those who had previously announced the coming of the Righteous One, whose betrayers and murderers you have now become; you who received the law as ordained by angels, and yet did not keep it.*
>
> Acts 7:51–53

Stephen's audience thought it was more spiritual to rend the garment than the heart. They loved paying such close attention to the details of the law of God that they missed the entire point and sinned against the law in the process. They resisted the Holy Spirit.

We can grieve the Holy Spirit

> *Let no unwholesome word proceed from your mouth, but only such a word as is good for edification according to the need of the moment, so that it will give grace to those who hear. Do not grieve the Holy Spirit of God, by whom you were sealed for the day of redemption. Let all bitterness and wrath and anger and clamor and slander be put away from you, along with all malice. Be kind to one another, tender-*

hearted, forgiving each other, just as God in Christ also has forgiven you.

> *Ephesians 4:29–32*

The church in Ephesus was made up of Jews and Gentiles— groups that traditionally did not mix well. In this letter, Paul strives with the people who were now charged to unite around the one faith. When they lived like those outside of Christ, when they insulted and held grudges against each other, they grieved the Holy Spirit.

We can insult the Holy Spirit

> *How much severer punishment do you think he will deserve who has trampled under foot the Son of God, and has regarded as unclean the blood of the covenant by which he was sanctified, and has **insulted the Spirit of grace**?*

> *Hebrews 10:29*

Arriving at this passage again, we see there is imminent judgment for the one who goes on sinning after receiving the knowledge of the truth. Those who have profaned the "blood of the covenant, which is poured out for many for forgiveness of sins" (Matthew 26:28) have insulted the Spirit of grace.

Every sin is a result of not taking God at His word. From the Garden until now, the proverbial fist has been shaken toward heaven: "We've heard your way; we'll do it our way." When we partake in that attitude, we lie to, resist, grieve, and insult God's Holy Spirit.

The study of the eternal sin is frequently loaded with concern. *Can I truly never be forgiven?* Let the words of Christ instruct and comfort you.

> *This is good and acceptable in the sight of God our Savior, who desires all men to be saved and to come to the knowledge of the truth.*

> *1 Timothy 2:3–4*

> *For this reason I endure all things for the sake of those who are chosen, so that they also may obtain the salvation which is in Christ Jesus and with it eternal glory. It is a*

trustworthy statement: For if we died with Him, we will also live with Him.

> *2 Timothy 2:10–11*

For you are all sons of God through faith in Christ Jesus. For all of you who were baptized into Christ have clothed yourselves with Christ.

> *Galatians 3:26–27*

This is the message we have heard from Him and announce to you, that God is Light, and in Him there is no darkness at all. If we say that we have fellowship with Him and yet walk in the darkness, we lie and do not practice the truth; but if we walk in the Light as He Himself is in the Light, we have fellowship with one another, and the blood of Jesus His Son cleanses us from all sin. If we say that we have no sin, we are deceiving ourselves and the truth is not in us. If we confess our sins, He is faithful and righteous to forgive us our sins and to cleanse us from all unrighteousness.

> *1 John 1:5–9*

Let us break the mold. Let us walk in the light, live in Christ, and fellowship in the joy of the Holy Spirit.

> *The grace of the Lord Jesus Christ, and the love of God, and the fellowship of the Holy Spirit, be with you all.*

> *2 Corinthians 13:14*

DISCUSSION QUESTIONS

1. What does it mean to blaspheme?

2. What does it mean to blaspheme the Holy Spirit?

3. Is it possible to blaspheme the Holy Spirit today?

4. What are other sins we can commit against the Spirit today?

5. What does it look like when people are committing such sins?

6. What stood out to you as particularly interesting or helpful in this chapter?

7. How does this study help you approach God with greater reverence?

DEEPER DEVOTION
www.cloudedbyemotion.com

11

WHAT IS THE INDWELLING OF THE HOLY SPIRIT?

The church's pastor paced back and forth in front of the stage, the band playing slowly in the background. "You have heard the message!" he yelled into the microphone.

"Amen!" came the audience's reply.

"Now, let us invite the Holy Spirit into our hearts tonight!" The pastor moved aside, and the band slowly increased their volume.

Lyrics showed on the screen for the church to follow along.

"Come, Holy Spirit; come! Set me on fire!"

I didn't sing along. Nor did the other four guys who were with me. We had been invited to a local church's "faith healing" service. About a hundred people were present, but no one came up to the front to be healed. That didn't stop the church from worshiping and inviting the Holy Spirit to "come."

The singing continued for another five minutes or so, repeating the same pleading words: "Come, Holy Spirit; come!"

Observing, I thought, *If these people have the relationship with God they claim to have, why is the Holy Spirit not already among them? Why does He have to "come"? Shouldn't He already be here?*

* * * * * * *

As we will see, there is a lot riding on whether or not God's Spirit dwells within us. The fact that the Holy Spirit indwells true believers is not in question in this chapter and the next. What is in question is this: What does it mean for the Holy Spirit to indwell a person?

> *However, you are not in the flesh but in the Spirit, if indeed*
> *the Spirit of God dwells in you. But if anyone does not have*
> *the Spirit of Christ, he does not belong to Him. If Christ is*
> *in you, though the body is dead because of sin, yet the spirit*
> *is alive because of righteousness. But if the Spirit of Him*
> *who raised Jesus from the dead dwells in you, He who*
> *raised Christ Jesus from the dead will also give life to your*
> *mortal bodies through His Spirit who dwells in you.*
>
> *Romans 8:9–11*

In this chapter, we will address these three questions:

1. When does the Holy Spirit indwell a person?
2. What blessings does the indwelling of the Holy Spirit provide?
3. What does it mean to be filled with the Holy Spirit?

WHEN DOES THE HOLY SPIRIT INDWELL A PERSON?

The Christian, having believed, is sealed with the Holy Spirit.

> *In Him, you also, after listening to the message of truth, the*
> *gospel of your salvation—**having also believed, you were***
> ***sealed in Him with the Holy Spirit of promise**, who is*
> *given as a pledge of our inheritance, with a view to the re-*
> *demption of God's own possession, to the praise of His*
> *glory.*
>
> *Ephesians 1:13–14*

We will return to this passage later to make some other ob-servations. The one thing that is clear at this point is one has to be a believer for the Spirit to be granted.

What does it mean to be a believer? There are many who would say someone who accepts the fact that Jesus is the Christ, the Son of God, qualifies as a believer. [1] But Scripture tells a dif-ferent story.

> *Nevertheless many even of the rulers believed in Him, but*

---

[1] This doctrine is frequently called "Salvation by Faith Alone." See Appen-dix.

> *because of the Pharisees they were not confessing Him, for*
> *fear that they would be put out of the synagogue; for they*
> *loved the approval of men rather than the approval of God.*
>
> *John 12:42–43*

These people believed. That is, they agreed in their minds Jesus was who He claimed to be, yet would the Scriptures call them *believers*? Were they people who truly had faith in Jesus? Would we expect the Holy Spirit of God to be within them?

Consider the demons as well.

> *When He came to the other side into the country of the*
> *Gadarenes, two men who were demon-possessed met Him*
> *as they were coming out of the tombs. They were so ex-*
> *tremely violent that no one could pass by that way. And*
> *they cried out, saying, "What business do we have with*
> *each other, Son of God? Have You come here to torment us*
> *before the time?"*
>
> *Matthew 8:28–29*

These demons were well aware of who Jesus was. They knew without a doubt—and even confessed—He was truly the Christ, the Son of God. Yet do we expect them to be granted eternal life in Jesus? Do we believe them to be led by the Spirit? No, as James would agree.

> *You believe that God is one. You do well; the demons also*
> *believe, and shudder. But are you willing to recognize, you*
> *foolish fellow, that faith without works is useless?*
>
> *James 2:19–20*

There's more to being a believer than simply acknowledging facts.

> *And he called for lights and rushed in, and trembling with*
> *fear he fell down before Paul and Silas, and after he*
> *brought them out, he said, "Sirs, what must I do to be*
> *saved?" They said, "Believe in the Lord Jesus, and you will*
> *be saved, you and your household." And they spoke the*
> *word of the Lord to him together with all who were in his*
> *house. And he took them that very hour of the night and*
> *washed their wounds, and immediately he was baptized,*

> *he and all his household. And he brought them into his house and set food before them, and rejoiced greatly, having believed in God with his whole household.*

> Acts 16:29–34

This jailer from Philippi was told to believe in verse 31, which is where many people stop reading or quoting. Yet he is not called a *believer* until verse 34, after placing his *faith* (the noun form of the verb *believe* in this verse) into Jesus. What happened between those verses? The jailer and his household listened to the word of God, he washed Paul and Silas' wounds (perhaps this was an act of repentance), and he and his household were baptized. Pay close attention to how Scripture describes baptism.

> *Or do you not know that all of us who have been baptized into Christ Jesus have been baptized into His death? Therefore we have been buried with Him through baptism into death, so that as Christ was raised from the dead through the glory of the Father, so we too might walk in newness of life. For if we have become united with Him in the likeness of His death, certainly we shall also be in the likeness of His resurrection, knowing this, that our old self was crucified with Him, in order that our body of sin might be done away with, so that we would no longer be slaves to sin; for he who has died is freed from sin.*

> Romans 6:3–7

A person who believes Jesus is the Christ will respond to Him as Lord, who commands all people to repent and be baptized.[2] Verse 5 says those who are made in the likeness of Jesus' death and burial through baptism have the assurance of a future resurrection. Two chapters later, Paul says:

> *But if the Spirit of Him who raised Jesus from the dead dwells in you, He who raised Christ Jesus from the dead will also give life to your mortal bodies through His Spirit*

---

[2] See Matthew 28:18–20 and Acts 2:38.

who dwells in you.

Romans 8:11

When does the Holy Spirit indwell a person? When that person becomes a child of God.

> *But as many as received Him, to them He gave the right to become children of God, even to those who believe in His name.*
>
> *John 1:12*

When a person believes in His name, that person is given the right to become God's child. Becoming God's child requires being born again in His name—not to earthly parents, but to a heavenly Father—which happens when the person is raised to walk a new life after being united with Jesus' death and burial in baptism.

> *Jesus answered and said to him* [Nicodemus], *"Truly, truly, I say to you, unless one is born again he cannot see the kingdom of God." Nicodemus said to Him, "How can a man be born when he is old? He cannot enter a second time into his mother's womb and be born, can he?" Jesus answered, "Truly, truly, I say to you, **unless one is born of water and the Spirit he cannot enter into the kingdom of God.**"*
>
> *John 3:3–5[3]*

WHAT BLESSINGS DOES THE HOLY SPIRIT'S INDWELLING PROVIDE?

It can be argued that most of the New Testament was written to answer this question. There were Christians who needed basic or additional teachings from the apostles and prophets; therefore, the epistles of the New Testament were written to teach Christians how to live by the Spirit.

> *In Him, you also, after listening to the message of truth, the gospel of your salvation—having also believed, you were sealed in Him with the Holy Spirit of promise, who is given*

---

[3] See also Titus 3:5–7.

> *as a pledge of our inheritance, with a view to the redemp-
> tion of God's own possession, to the praise of His glory.*
> *Ephesians 1:13–14*

The Holy Spirit is given to the believer as a promise—a pledge—of inheritance. It is normal for Christians today to say "I am saved," or "I was saved when…" Although that is language used in the Scriptures (even in the next chapter in Ephesians), the New Testament speaks more of a *future* salvation.[4] Though my sins have been forgiven in Jesus Christ, I still look forward to when He returns to *save* me from temptation and death. There is a present sense of salvation, but there is much more to come. For the time being, I have the *pledge* (some translations say *guarantee*, others *down payment* or *earnest*) of the Holy Spirit.

The Spirit has been given by the promise of God, and I know He will not break that promise. What does that say to those who have the habit of praying or pleading for the Holy Spirit to "come"? It is unreasonable and unscriptural to think about the Holy Spirit coming and going, over and over, the way some churches indicate. If God has provided His Spirit (He has), then I do not need to pray for the Holy Spirit to "come" on a regular basis, whether I'm within the Christian assembly or alone.

Even though the New Testament is filled with information regarding the Holy Spirit's role in our lives, Romans 8 might be the richest passage. I recommend you pause to read it now. In that chapter, we learn the indwelling of the Holy Spirit gives life to our spirits. Without the work of Jesus, I would be condemned to death by law. The Spirit of God provides life where there was death. And He provides peace where there was hostility. Again, that happens when we die to sin through repentance and baptism, when the Spirit of God causes us to be born again to a living hope. How else could we expect to be raised to newness of life if we have not crucified the old self?[5]

> *For all who are being led by the Spirit of God, these are sons*

---

[4] See Romans 13:11 and 1 Peter 1:6–9.
[5] See also Romans 6:3–7; Galatians 2:20; 1 Peter 1:3–5, and 22–25.

> *of God. For you have not received a spirit of slavery leading*
> *to fear again, but you have received a spirit of adoption as*
> *sons by which we cry out, "Abba! Father!" The Spirit Him-*
> *self testifies with our spirit that we are children of God, and*
> *if children, heirs also, heirs of God and fellow heirs with*
> *Christ, if indeed we suffer with Him so that we may also be*
> *glorified with Him.*
>
> *Romans 8:14–17*

In addition to the leading of the Holy Spirit, which we will focus on in the next chapter, this passage says the Spirit testifies *with* (not *to*) our personal spirits that we are God's children. How? Earlier in this chapter Paul contrasts those who set their minds on the flesh with those who set their minds on the Spirit. When a believer has the indwelling of the Spirit, that person has heeded the call of the gospel. There is no question where he belongs: in Christ, where there is no condemnation; he has life as a child of God. We know (and therefore, testify) that we have obeyed the gospel—if, indeed, we have. So does the Spirit.

> *In the same way the Spirit also helps our weakness; for we*
> *do not know how to pray as we should, but the Spirit Him-*
> *self intercedes for us with groanings too deep for words; and*
> *He who searches the hearts knows what the mind of the*
> *Spirit is, because He intercedes for the saints according to*
> *the will of God.*
>
> *Romans 8:26–27*

What a blessing God provides through His Spirit—the ability to communicate to the Author of the universe clearly, even if we ourselves do not know how to articulate what needs to be said! The Spirit helps the prayers of the believer "according to the will of God."

Another blessing that comes with the indwelling of God's Spirit is life in His family.

> *Do you not know that you are a temple of God and that*
> *the Spirit of God dwells in you? If any man destroys the*
> *temple of God, God will destroy him, for the temple of God*
> *is holy, and that is what you are.*

1 Corinthians 3:16–17

Three chapters later, Paul refers to each individual Christian as the temple of the Holy Spirit (this concept will be studied more in the next chapter), but in this passage, he is talking about the entire church. The pronoun *you* is plural. The entire church makes up the temple of the Holy Spirit.[6]

Consider the role of the temple in the Old Testament. It was the place of fellowship with God and other members of Israel. It was the place to serve God through giving and sacrifice. It was the place to appeal to God for forgiveness. It was a place of prayer. It was the place where God's glory *dwelt*.

Since the cross, however, the veil of the temple has been torn.[7] The religious system that required God's people to worship in a specific geographical location and within a specific building is no longer in place.[8] Instead, Jews and Gentiles are welcomed into His presence through Christ and as the church—not a building, but a *people*. That people is where God chooses to *dwell* today through His Spirit.

> *And coming to Him as to a living stone which has been rejected by men, but is choice and precious in the sight of God, you also, as living stones, are being built up as a spiritual house for a holy priesthood, to offer up spiritual sacrifices acceptable to God through Jesus Christ.*

1 Peter 2:4–5

God's Spirit is more active in our lives than we will ever know before the final resurrection. In the activities that are revealed to us, some aspects of them are left to the secret things of God.[9]

What blessings come with God's indwelling Spirit? Of the countless blessings, we have noted the "down payment" of salvation, spiritual life, confirmation of adoption, help in prayer, and fellowship with God and His people in His temple (the church). If these blessings are yours, do you thank God for them

---

[6] Compare with Ephesians 2:19–22; 1 Timothy 3:14–15; and 1 Peter 2:4–10.
[7] See Matthew 27:50–51; Hebrews 8:6–13; and 9:15–17.
[8] See John 4:20–24.
[9] See Deuteronomy 29:29.

every day?

> *Blessed be the God and Father of our Lord Jesus Christ,*
> *who has blessed us with every spiritual blessing in the heav-*
> *enly places in Christ.*
>
> *Ephesians 1:3*

WHAT DOES IT MEAN TO BE FILLED WITH THE HOLY SPIRIT?

In Ephesians 5:18, the apostle Paul tells Christians to "be filled with the Spirit." What does that mean, and how does it work?

Being filled with or being full of Holy Spirit is explicitly mentioned over a dozen times in the New Testament. All but one of them are within the writings of Luke (the gospel of Luke and the book of Acts). In those cases, being filled with the Holy Spirit was something beyond the person's control. For instance, John the Baptist was "filled with the Holy Spirit while yet in his mother's womb" (Luke 1:15). John's father was able to prophecy once he was "filled with the Holy Spirit" (Luke 1:67). When Mary greeted Elizabeth while carrying Jesus in her womb, Elizabeth was then "filled with the Holy Spirit" (Luke 1:41). In Acts 2:4, the apostles were "filled with the Holy Spirit" when they were baptized with the Holy Spirit. In most of the cases when Luke mentions that someone was filled with the Spirit, it precedes some type of Spirit-inspired speech—whether praise to God, the gospel to sinners, motivation to disciples, or condemnation to the guilty.[10] But none of the accounts are obedience to a commandment to "be filled with the Spirit."

The one time outside of Luke's writing that being filled with the Spirit is mentioned is when Paul commands it to Christians in Ephesians 5:18. Being filled with the Spirit is a commandment in that passage alone. Therefore, to understand what Paul means in Ephesians 5:18, a comparison of Colossians 3:16–17 is a better approach than a comparison of a passage in Luke or Acts, where

---

[10] See also Acts 4:8, 31; 7:55; and 13:9–12.

being filled with the Spirit is not a commandment, but an event. Consider the similarity between these two passages:

> *And do not get drunk with wine, for that is dissipation, but* **be filled with the Spirit,** *speaking to one another in psalms and hymns and spiritual songs, singing and making melody with your heart to the Lord; always giving thanks for all things in the name of our Lord Jesus Christ to God, even the Father.*
>
> *Ephesians 5:18–20*
>
> **Let the word of Christ richly dwell within you,** *with all wisdom teaching and admonishing one another with psalms and hymns and spiritual songs, singing with thankfulness in your hearts to God. Whatever you do in word or deed, do all in the name of the Lord Jesus, giving thanks through Him to God the Father.*
>
> *Colossians 3:16–17*

If these two passages are meant to complement each other, then being filled with the Spirit is the same as letting the word of Christ richly dwell within. Note a few things about these passages with me.

First, Paul had already reminded the Christians of Ephesus that they were sealed with the Holy Spirit of promise (Ephesians 1:13–14). In other words, they were already enjoying the blessings of the indwelling of the Holy Spirit. Yet Paul still commanded them to "be filled with the Spirit." Had the Spirit or the promise of God departed from them between chapters 1 and 5 of Ephesians? Certainly not. Yet there was a dimension of the Spirit's work that could still be improved on by obeying the commandment to "be filled with the Spirit."

When Paul essentially told the Colossians to do the same thing, he told them, "Let the word of Christ richly dwell within you." Therefore, understanding and application of God's word, at least in this context, fulfills the commandment to "be filled with the Spirit." Paul also explained that this is compounded through giving thanks to God and teaching each other through singing. The more thankful, and the more taught a person is, the more *filled with the Spirit* he may be.

In addition to that, it is also worth noting that the imperative to "be filled with the Spirit" comes directly after Paul had this to say:

> *Therefore be careful how you walk, not as unwise men but as wise, making the most of your time, because the days are evil. So then do not be foolish, but understand what the will of the Lord is. And do not get drunk with wine, for that is dissipation, but be filled with the Spirit.*
>
> *Ephesians 5:15–18*

The four-fold commandment, then, is:

1. Do not be foolish.
2. Understand the *Lord's will*.
3. Do not get drunk.
4. Be *filled with the Spirit*.

All of this makes the connection of the Holy Spirit's work within us through His revealed word conceptually connected with an unbreakable bond. We will continue to explore this idea in the next chapter. But for now, do not be foolish, but let the word of Christ dwell within you. In other words, be filled with the Holy Spirit of God.

DISCUSSION QUESTIONS

1. When does the Holy Spirit begin to indwell a person?

2. What do the Scriptures mean when they refer to someone who truly believes?

3. What blessings are available to the people who have the indwelling of the Holy Spirit?

4. How can believers be confident the Spirit dwells within them?

5. How can we obey the commandment to be filled with the Spirit?

6. What stood out to you as particularly interesting or helpful in this chapter?

7. How does this study help you approach God with greater reverence?

DEEPER DEVOTION
www.cloudedbyemotion.com

12

HOW DOES THE HOLY SPIRIT LEAD AND INDWELL A BELIEVER?

In an effort to "examine everything carefully; hold fast to that which is good" (1 Thessalonians 5:21), I read the Book of Mormon in its entirety in 2015. Having completed that exercise, I was not hesitant to accept an opportunity to study with the next members of The Church of Jesus Christ of Latter-day Saints who came to my door.

At the end of the Book of Mormon, Moroni 10:4–5 says:

> *And when ye shall receive these things, I would exhort you that ye would ask God, the Eternal Father, in the name of Christ, if these things are not true; and if ye shall ask with a sincere heart, with real intent, having faith in Christ, he will manifest the truth of it unto you,* **by the power of the Holy Ghost***. And* **by the power of the Holy Ghost ye may know the truth of all things***.

Looking at this passage with the LDS "elders" who had come to my home to study with me, I asked, "Have you followed through with this?"

"Yes," they both said in unison.

"That must have been a special moment," I said.

They agreed.

"Jacob, how is it the power of the Holy Ghost convinced you the Book of Mormon is from God?" I was sure to ask the question carefully, not wanting to set him up for a trap, and not wanting to come off condescending.

"I was in my bedroom," he began, "and I prayed to Heavenly Father to help me know the truth. Suddenly, my arms were filled with goosebumps, and I felt a shiver up my spine."

"Wow! Sounds intense!" I said.

"It was."

"What about you, Tyler?"

"It was similar to Jacob. My dad and I had just finished reading a part of the Book of Mormon, and he said it was time for me to receive my own faith. He had me go up to my room and ask Heavenly Father if all of this is true. When I did, my feet felt like they were on fire—like really on *fire*. I had to look down to convince myself they weren't! Even though there were no flames, I started sweating like crazy."

"This is all very interesting to me." I paused. "I'm not going to try to discount your personal experiences, guys. I wouldn't want you to do that to me. Our experiences—especially ones we connect with God—are important to us. But I have a serious question."

"Sure," Jacob said. "What is it?"

"A few years ago, I was part of an Apostolic Church, and the members there said they received the Holy Ghost. Afterward, they started running around the building, losing control of their bodies, and claiming they could speak in tongues. I was as curious about that as I am about this passage here in the Book of Mormon. So, I asked them the same thing: How is it you *know* you have God's blessing in this? My Apostolic friends said the same thing—warm, tingly feelings and goosebumps."

There was silence for a moment.

"I guess I have two questions," I continued. "How can we know these feelings really are the work of God? And if they truly are from God, why is He approving of two different religions?

Jacob's words said what Tyler's facial expression was already saying. "Good questions. I've never really thought about that."

* * * * * * *

I still have not received answers to those questions from my Mormon friends. I recently encountered this concept again when reading some online reviews of a new television series about the life of Christ. One viewer said, "[I was] so touched and moved I cried throughout every Episode! So many Holy Spirit goosebumps along the way!"

When the Holy Spirit indwells a believer, what is it like? How does it feel? How is it confirmed? How does the Holy Spirit lead His people? When we ask these questions, we are connecting all the dots from the previous studies.

- The Holy Spirit is not some impersonal force, but He is God Almighty who is deeply concerned for your soul (Chapter 1).
- The Spirit was sent to guide the apostles and prophets in order to reveal and be an additional witness to the soul-saving gospel to mankind (Chapter 2).
- The Holy Spirit provided amazing, undeniable miracles in the first century to confirm the words of the apostles and prophets, which have been preserved for us in the form of the Scriptures (Chapter 3).
- Miraculous gifts of the Holy Spirit were imparted after Jesus' death and resurrection through baptism with the Holy Spirit and laying on of the apostles' hands (Chapters 5, 6, and 7).
- God's Spirit provided the gifts of tongues, prophecy, and knowledge to convey His gospel while the church was in its infancy and without access to the completed Scriptures (Chapters 8 and 9).
- Jesus takes the role of the Holy Spirit's work through miracles and the gospel of the kingdom seriously, and we should too (Chapter 10).
- God has provided His pledge of inheritance upon those who have heard and obeyed the gospel of Jesus Christ (Chapter 11).

What is the chain that binds all of this together? Because He is deeply concerned for our souls, the Holy Spirit has gone to miraculous measures so you and I can have access to God's word, which will guide us to eternal life.

For I am not ashamed of the gospel, for it is the power of

> *God for salvation to everyone who believes, to the Jew first and also to the Greek. For in it the righteousness of God is revealed from faith to faith; as it is written, "But the righteous man shall live by faith."*
>
> *Romans 1:16–17*

Hardly a day goes by for me when I do not meet a religious person who claims to believe in the Father, the Son, and the Holy Spirit, yet he or she lacks basic understanding of the Scriptures. The description, "biblical illiteracy," comes to mind. For someone who is a Christian, is it possible to overestimate the value of the words the Holy Spirit moved holy men to utter?[1]

Since God's power for the most important task of human history is active within the gospel of Jesus, there is no wonder why the word of God is called "the sword of the Spirit" in Ephesians 6. Though swords can be used for defense, the sword of the Spirit is the only part of the full armor of God listed in that passage that can be considered an offensive weapon. Also unique is that the sword of the Spirit is the only one explicitly defined for us. We are to take up the "sword of the Spirit, *which is the word of God*" (v. 17). If it hadn't been defined for us by the Spirit's inspiration, people would certainly come up with many different "mystical" interpretations of what the Holy Spirit's sword is and how to wield it. However, we can thank God it is not left to us to guess. It is the powerful word of God. And even the sharpest physical sword falls short of the power of God's word.

> *For the word of God is living and active and sharper than any two-edged sword, and piercing as far as the division of soul and spirit, of both joints and marrow, and able to judge the thoughts and intentions of the heart. And there is no creature hidden from His sight, but all things are open and laid bare to the eyes of Him with whom we have to do.*
>
> *Hebrews 4:12–13*

With that introduction in mind, let us consider the first main question of this chapter.

---

[1] See 2 Timothy 3:13–17 and 2 Peter 1:16–21.

HOW DOES THE HOLY SPIRIT LEAD A BELIEVER?

There is a striking difference between what the Scriptures mean by being "led by the Spirit" and what many religious people mean by that phrase today. It is popular to hear people claim to be led by the Spirit while deciding on who to marry, what job to take, where to go to school, or whether or not to buy a house (or a sandwich, for that matter).

There are two passages of Scripture that say Christians are led by the Spirit of God. In both cases, being led by the Spirit is directly contrasted with being led by deeds of the flesh.[2]

> *But I say, **walk by the Spirit**, and you will not carry out the desire of the flesh. For the flesh sets its desire against the Spirit, and the Spirit against the flesh; for these are in opposition to one another, so that you may not do the things that you please. But **if you are led by the Spirit**, you are not under the Law. Now the deeds of the flesh are evident, which are: immorality, impurity, sensuality, idolatry, sorcery, enmities, strife, jealousy, outbursts of anger, disputes, dissensions, factions, envying, drunkenness, carousing, and things like these, of which I forewarn you, just as I have forewarned you, that those who practice such things will not inherit the kingdom of God. But **the fruit of the Spirit** is love, joy, peace, patience, kindness, goodness, faithfulness, gentleness, self-control; against such things there is no law. Now those who belong to Christ Jesus have crucified the flesh with its passions and desires. **If we live by the Spirit, let us also walk by the Spirit**. Let us not become boastful, challenging one another, envying one another.*
>
> *Galatians 5:16–26*

Keeping in step with the Spirit means being led by the Spirit, which has to do with *our* choice to follow His revealed will, and not the Spirit coming into our lives and making our choices for us. It is evident that we are led by the Spirit when we follow the

---

[2] Carefully compare Romans 8:4 with Galatians 5:16; Romans 8:14 with Galatians 5:18; and Romans 8:13 with Galatians 5:19–21.

Spirit's directives, including producing the fruit of the Spirit, which is "love, joy, peace, patience, kindness, goodness, faithfulness, gentleness, self-control."

Note—these qualities are not miraculous. God does not need to defy natural laws for you and me to be loving and kind people. When the Holy Spirit leads a person, He does not control a person's life in some puppeteering way. Instead, the more a person spends in the word of God, allowing it to shape his heart, mind, and life, that person will exhibit such things. The Scriptures provide instructions, commandments, principles, and examples for being loving; being joyful; peacemaking; long-suffering; being kind; doing good; walking by faith; exhibiting meekness; and self-controlling the mind, heart, and body. In every situation we find ourselves, there is an opportunity for the Spirit to lead us. The Spirit works through the Scriptures to develop the type of lifestyle God expects from His children. The Spirit will bear His fruit in the believer's life.

It has always been the case that as people come closer to the will of God, when they understand His true nature, love, and intentions, that their hearts soften. Look at God's perspective of what happens when someone is convicted and repents and turns back to Him.

> *And I will give them one heart, and put a new spirit within them. And I will take the heart of stone out of their flesh and give them a heart of flesh, that they may walk in My statutes and keep My ordinances and do them. Then they will be My people, and I shall be their God.*
>
> *Ezekiel 11:19–20*

It is common to hear religious people claim the Holy Spirit comes into a person's heart to interpret and understand the Scriptures. They claim that without the "prodding," "enlightening," "illuminating," or "leading" of the Holy Spirit on a person in some direct way, that person will never understand or believe the Scriptures, nor will he or she be "drawn" to Jesus. A prooftext often used is John 16:7–15, in which Jesus says:

> *But I tell you the truth, it is to your advantage that I go*

away; for if I do not go away, the Helper will not come to you; but if I go, I will send Him to you. And He, when He comes, will convict the world concerning sin and righteousness and judgment; concerning sin, because they do not believe in Me; and concerning righteousness, because I go to the Father and you no longer see Me; and concerning judgment, because the ruler of this world has been judged. I have many more things to say to you, but you cannot bear them now. But when He, the Spirit of truth, comes, He will guide you into all the truth; for He will not speak on His own initiative, but whatever He hears, He will speak; and He will disclose to you what is to come. He will glorify Me, for He will take of Mine and will disclose it to you. All things that the Father has are Mine; therefore I said that He takes of Mine and will disclose it to you.

As noted in Chapter 2 of this book, this passage is among the most misapplied passages in all of Scripture. The primary reason is that people forget to ask the basic questions of interpretation:

1. Who is speaking?
2. To whom is that person speaking?

In this case, Jesus is speaking to the apostles. In chapters 14–16 of the gospel of John, Jesus provides the apostles with warnings and promises which would be fulfilled after His resurrection. These men would soon be commissioned to take the gospel to the entire world. Thankfully, they did not have to rely on their fallible memories, but instead, they relied on Jesus' promise that He would send the inspiration of the Holy Spirit, who would lead them to all truth and bring to their memories all Jesus had taught them.[3]

The result of all of this, of course, was the public and private preaching of the apostles and prophets and the production of the New Testament Scriptures. Today, centuries later, the Holy Spirit continues to "convict the world concerning sin and righteousness and judgment" (John 16:8) with His sword, the word of God. He still saves people through "the gospel, for it is the

---

[3] Compare John 16:7–15 and Matthew 28:19–20.

power of God for salvation to everyone who believes" (Romans 1:16).

The Holy Spirit does not operate on a person's heart directly apart from the Scriptures. To assert that the Spirit is working outside of the Scriptures to directly convert the sinner or bring the believer to repentance is to nullify the sufficiency of the gospel of Jesus. Consider, for example, the man traveling from Jerusalem back to Ethiopia in Acts 8.

> But an angel of the Lord spoke to Philip saying, "Get up and go south to the road that descends from Jerusalem to Gaza." (This is a desert road.) So he got up and went; and there was an Ethiopian eunuch, a court official of Candace, queen of the Ethiopians, who was in charge of all her treasure; and he had come to Jerusalem to worship, and he was returning and sitting in his chariot, and was reading the prophet Isaiah. Then the Spirit said to Philip, "Go up and join this chariot."
>
> Acts 8:26–29

If there ever was a perfect time for the Holy Spirit to speak directly to a sinner to convict him or come into his heart to "enlighten" him, this was it. But that's not what happened. Nowhere in Scripture does the Holy Spirit directly teach a sinner the gospel. Who did the Spirit speak to on this occasion? Philip, who was appointed to preach Jesus to the Ethiopian man using the word of God.

> Then Philip opened his mouth, and beginning from this Scripture he preached Jesus to him. As they went along the road they came to some water; and the eunuch said, "Look! Water! What prevents me from being baptized?"
>
> Acts 8:35–36[4]

Likewise, reading through the account in Acts 2 of the first

---

[4] Compare this account with the accounts of Saul in Acts 9 and Cornelius in Acts 10. In both cases, the Lord spoke directly to the messengers (Ananias and Peter, respectively) to ensure the message was delivered, but He left it up to them to deliver the message. He did not send the Holy Spirit directly on those who needed to hear the gospel.

sermon after the resurrection of Christ, we see the emphasis on audibly hearing (or in later cases, reading) the gospel through words (not a quiet voice within the heart).

- "And they [the apostles] were all filled with the Holy Spirit and began to *speak* with other tongues, as the Spirit was giving them *utterance*" (v. 4).
- "Each one of them was *hearing* them *speak* in his own language" (v. 6).
- "We each *hear* them in our own language to which we were born" (v. 8).
- "We *hear* them in our own tongues *speaking* of the mighty deeds of God" (v. 11).
- "But Peter, taking his stand with the eleven, raised his *voice* and *declared* to them: 'Men of Judea and all you who live in Jerusalem, let this be known to you and give heed to my *words*'" (v. 14).
- "Men of Israel, *listen* to these *words*" (v. 22).
- "Now when they *heard* this, they were pierced to the heart" (v. 37).
- "Peter *said* to them, "Repent, and each of you be baptized in the name of Jesus Christ'" (v. 38).
- "And with many other *words* he solemnly testified and kept on exhorting them, *saying*, 'Be saved from this perverse generation'" (v. 40).
- "So then, those who had *received his word* were baptized" (v. 41).
- "They were continually devoting themselves to the *apostles' teaching*" (v. 42).

If the Holy Spirit comes directly into a person's heart to interpret or to convict the sinner, why the emphasis of hearing the spoken words of the gospel? What would be the purpose of the teachers or the Scriptures in the first place?

Since the word of God is the work of the Spirit, God's Spirit will never lead someone to do something outside of or beyond the Scriptures.[5] To be led by the Holy Spirit simply, but profoundly, means to diligently study and apply God's word to your life.[6]

Can you echo the words of Psalm 119:105?

Your word is a lamp to my feet
And a light to my path.

Again, many sincere religious people talk about "feeling" the work or leading of the Holy Spirit, and some believe goosebumps to be evidence of the Spirit's work in their lives. If that is true, then what are we to make of the many false, incompatible religions that have also claimed feelings are the source of God's (or some other god's) truth? The Scriptures of the true God warn people over and over *not* to trust subjective feelings, not to follow the heart.

The heart is more deceitful than all else
And is desperately sick;
Who can understand it?

Jeremiah 17:9[7]

Nowhere does Scripture say anything about emotionally experiencing the Holy Spirit. No one in the Bible talks about goosebumps or emotions in the context of the leading of the Holy Spirit. So, if you have been taught you can feel the work of the Holy Spirit, then the person teaching you was not teaching from the Scriptures. In other words, that person was not being

---

[5] In the beginning, the middle, and the end of the Scriptures, the Holy Spirit warns the recipients of God's word to never add to or take away from the Scriptures. See Deuteronomy 4:2; Proverbs 30:6; and Revelation 22:18–19. Doing so will prove someone a liar. If someone claims to revere God's word, and yet tampers with it, he is lying. Claiming the Holy Spirit leads someone beyond His own word would also be accusing God's Spirit of lying.

[6] James exhorts his audience to ask for wisdom from God in James 1:5–8. He then explains how people are tempted and carried away by their own lusts (vv. 12–15). Then, he reminds the Christian that the Father of lights has provided His good and perfect gift—the law of liberty through Christ—which can prevent our deception (vv. 16–20). Finally, he urges the reader to do God's will, receiving "the word implanted" (vv. 22–25). Doing so will allow us to see in a mirror clearly (cf. 1 Corinthians 13:9–12).

[7] See also Jeremiah 10:23 and Proverbs 28:26.

led by the Holy Spirit. Instead of through *feelings* in the heart, God's indwelling Spirit works to strengthen the believer through *faith*.

> *For this reason I bow my knees before the Father, from whom every family in heaven and on earth derives its name, that He would grant you, according to the riches of His glory, to **be strengthened with power through His Spirit in the inner man, so that Christ may dwell in your hearts through faith**; and that you, being rooted and grounded in love, may be able to comprehend with all the saints what is the breadth and length and height and depth, and to know the love of Christ which surpasses knowledge, that you may be filled up to all the fullness of God.*
>
> *Ephesians 3:14–19*[8]

Faith is the substructure of our hope; it is based upon reasonable understanding of who God is.[9] Don't get me wrong; to know God's Spirit dwells within me makes me feel great! Sometimes I am overwhelmed with emotion when worshiping God, while praying, while reading His word, while fellowshipping with His family, and while thinking of His love for me. The heart is not removed from the equation. It's simply put in the right place: in subjection to God's objective authority. So, when God's word tells me the Spirit dwells within me, I believe that fact, I *know* it, through *faith*, not through *feelings*. That faith is produced by hearing the word of God.

> *So faith comes from hearing, and hearing by the word of Christ.*
>
> *Romans 10:17*

Someone might ask, "Then how will I know God's will for my life, if He does not lead me through my feelings?" As has

---

[8] In context, we "may be able to comprehend with all the saints" all that Paul discusses in this passage by reading what he wrote, which was revealed in the Spirit (see vv. 1–5). This is another passage that gives us confidence that God has provided in the Scriptures all He wants us to know.

[9] See Hebrews 11:1, 6.

been emphasized all along, God's will has already been revealed to you in His Scriptures. Read Matthew 7:21–27 slowly and carefully. As far as the "big" decisions in life go, like job offers, major purchases, relationships, and so on, meditate on these Scriptures:

> *And we know that God causes all things to work together for good to those who love God, to those who are called according to His purpose.*
>
> *Romans 8:28*
>
> *Come now, you who say, "Today or tomorrow we will go to such and such a city, and spend a year there and engage in business and make a profit." Yet you do not know what your life will be like tomorrow. You are just a vapor that appears for a little while and then vanishes away. Instead, you ought to say, "If the Lord wills, we will live and also do this or that."*
>
> *James 4:13–15*

God desires for your life to be filled with joy. But sometimes our preconceived ideas of joy do not match God's definitions. For instance, the Christians in Thessalonica learned "the joy of the Holy Spirit" through tribulation, not physical prosperity (see 1 Thessalonians 1:6). The Scriptures do not tell you to wait for the Holy Spirit to prod your heart in any given direction. Go ahead and plan and make prayerful decisions, considering how your choices will glorify God and affect your and others' relationships with God. Know that every decision is contingent on whether or not God has other plans. Learn the lesson of the rich fool:

> *And He told them a parable, saying, "The land of a rich man was very productive. And he began reasoning to himself, saying, 'What shall I do, since I have no place to store my crops?' Then he said, 'This is what I will do: I will tear down my barns and build larger ones, and there I will store all my grain and my goods. And I will say to my soul, "Soul, you have many goods laid up for many years to come; take your ease, eat, drink and be merry."' But God said to him,*

'You fool! This very night your soul is required of you; and now who will own what you have prepared?' So is the man who stores up treasure for himself, and is not rich toward God."

Luke 12:16–21

God's people are chosen "according to the foreknowledge of God the Father, by the sanctifying work of the Spirit, to obey Jesus Christ and be sprinkled with His blood" (1 Peter 1:2). If the Spirit comes down on people and changes their hearts without the understanding and conviction of the Scriptures, then what is the point of the Scriptures? The Spirit certainly sanctifies the person from the inside out. He teaches, reproves, corrects, and trains. According to Jesus, that happens through God's word.

Sanctify them in the truth; Your word is truth.

John 17:17

All Scripture is inspired by God and profitable for teaching, for reproof, for correction, for training in righteousness; so that the man of God may be adequate, equipped for every good work.

2 Timothy 3:16–17

Once again, consider when God's glory filled His temple in the Old Testament.

The priests could not enter into the house of the LORD because the glory of the LORD filled the LORD's house. All the sons of Israel, seeing the fire come down and the glory of the LORD upon the house, bowed down on the pavement with their faces to the ground, and they worshiped and gave praise to the LORD, saying, "Truly He is good, truly His lovingkindness is everlasting."

2 Chronicles 7:2–3

Now, consider how that blessing is available to every heart today. The Holy Spirit dwells within His temple—the church, the members of Christ's body. Don't you want that for your life? Don't you yearn for God to make His home within your heart? The Scriptures say this happens for those who listen to His commandments with an open heart, obey His word, and die to self and sin through repentance and baptism into Him and into His body (the church).[10] If you have not done that, do not delay in your obedience.

HOW DOES THE HOLY SPIRIT DWELL WITHIN THE BELIEVER?

There are things about God and the spiritual world we will never know, at least before the final resurrection. I wonder if the answer to this question is one of them. There have been many different answers presented in formal debates, lectures, and books on how the Holy Spirit dwells within His people.

One thing we should note right away is that this was not an issue with first-century Christians. This was not a debate the apostles and prophets spoke to. To the contrary, by asking "do you not know...?" the apostle Paul seems to indicate that knowing *that* the Spirit dwells within the church and within the individual is enough, and knowing *how* is somewhat irrelevant.

> **Do you not know** that you are a temple of God and that the Spirit of God dwells in you?
>
> *1 Corinthians 3:19[11]*
>
> Or **do you not know** that your body is a temple of the Holy Spirit who is in you, whom you have from God, and that you are not your own?
>
> *1 Corinthians 6:19[12]*

The Scriptures simply state that the Spirit dwells within the believer and leaves it at that; therefore:

1. A perfect understanding of the answer to this question is not necessary to receive the blessings of the indwelling of the Spirit.
2. If two faithful Christians disagree on the answer to this

---

[10] See Romans 6:1–7; 1 Corinthians 12:12–13; Ephesians 1:22–23; 5:23; 1 John 3:24; and 4:12.

[11] In this passage, "you" is plural and is a reference to the church as a whole, not the individual believer.

[12] In this passage, "you" is singular and is a reference to the individual believer.

one question, they can continue to be brethren in the faith.

When attempting to answer this question, many have isolated the Holy Spirit from the rest of deity. Is the Holy Spirit promised to dwell within the believer? Certainly. But so are the Father and the Son. Jesus told the apostles:

> *"I will ask the Father, and He will give you another Helper, that He may be with you forever; that is the Spirit of truth, whom the world cannot receive, because it does not see Him or know Him, but you know Him because* **He** [the Holy Spirit] ***abides with you and will be in you.*** *I will not leave you as orphans; I will come to you. After a little while the world will no longer see Me, but you will see Me; because I live, you will live also.* **In that day you will know that I am in My Father, and you in Me, and I in you.** *He who has My commandments and keeps them is the one who loves Me; and he who loves Me will be loved by My Father, and I will love him and will disclose Myself to him." Judas (not Iscariot) said to Him, "Lord, what then has happened that You are going to disclose Yourself to us and not to the world?" Jesus answered and said to him,* **"If anyone loves Me, he will keep My word; and My Father will love him, and We will come to him and make Our abode with him."**

> *John 14:16–23*

In this passage, Jesus says the Holy Spirit will be *with* and *in* the apostles. As we have seen, this promise is provided to all of God's children in other passages.[13] Jesus also says that He and the Father will make their abode within the ones who keep His word.[14] How simple, yet how profound! God—the Father, the

---

[13] See Romans 8:1–27; Galatians 4:6; and 2 Timothy 1:13–14.

[14] In previous applications of this passage and surrounding ones, we have noticed that Jesus was speaking directly to the apostles; therefore, we should be careful not to assume His promises to *you* are directly to *me* or *us*. However, Jesus shifts His promises from to "you" (the apostles) to anyone "who has my commandments and keeps them." Thank God that we *do* have his commandments! Are we keeping them?

Son, and the Holy Spirit—promises to take up residence within the ones who listen to, trust, and obey His teachings. This abiding is reciprocal. We can abide in God, and He can abide in us.

> *I do not ask on behalf of these* [apostles] *alone, but for those also who believe in Me through their word; that they may all be one;* **even as You, Father, are in Me and I in You, that they also may be in Us,** *so that the world may believe that You sent Me.*
>
> *John 17:20–21*
>
> *This is His commandment, that we believe in the name of His Son Jesus Christ, and love one another, just as He commanded us.* **The one who keeps His commandments abides in Him, and He in him.** *We know by this that He abides in us, by the Spirit whom He has given us.*
>
> *1 John 3:23–24*

So, how does the Holy Spirit dwell within the believer? While we know some of the facts, only God knows the specifics. It is more than acceptable for us to not fully understand exactly how God dwells in His people. Perhaps one of the reasons we pursue the answer to such questions is we want complete explanations for the way God works in our lives, as if we are entitled to the secret things of God. That is not what the Scriptures are for.

> *The secret things belong to the* LORD *our God, but the things revealed belong to us and to our sons forever, that we may observe all the words of this law.*
>
> *Deuteronomy 29:29*

As these words applied directly to the children of Israel, they may still be applied to us in principle today. Let us leave the secret things to God, but let us pursue and observe with all our hearts what He has revealed. Continue to study and apply God's word to your life with faith. In other words, be led by the Spirit.

As I close this chapter, let me reiterate one thing. The Holy Spirit certainly dwells within God's children. But we must remember that the Scriptures do not make miraculous gifts, feelings, or emotions the test of whether or not someone has the indwelling of the Holy Spirit. No one needs to prophesy or miraculously speak in other languages to prove he has the Spirit within him. We do not need to fall into a trance or begin convulsing before we can know God has fulfilled His promise. We can know, because God has promised His indwelling through the condition of receiving and obeying His commandments. Have you done so?

> *But if the Spirit of Him who raised Jesus from the dead dwells in you, He who raised Christ Jesus from the dead will also give life to your mortal bodies through His Spirit who dwells in you.*
>
> *Romans 8:11*

DISCUSSION QUESTIONS

1. What is your response to the concept that God's Spirit is available to all mankind today?

2. Being led by the Spirit is in contrast to what?

3. Being led by the Spirit is equated with what?

4. How is someone led by the Spirit? How is that different to how many people in the religious world teach on this subject today?

5. What stood out to you as particularly interesting or helpful in this chapter?

6. How does this study help you approach God with greater reverence?

*DEEPER
DEVOTION
www.cloudedbyemotion.com*

13

SO WHAT?

Trevor looked off into the distance as he began his story. "When I was called to ministry—when I was baptized with the Holy Spirit—I forsook everything. I left my home. I left my job. I packed my suitcase, and I moved to a different city. Other Christians took me in, and I lived off of their generosity."

Trevor, along with Lloyd, was leading a local group of people who met in a home to worship God in Newtown, Wellington, New Zealand. They were a quiet group, unlike my friends in the Apostolic Church. My co-worker John and I had started meeting with Trevor and Lloyd on a weekly basis to study the Bible and enjoy some coffee together.

"What do you mean you were baptized with the Holy Spirit?" John asked before taking a sip of his coffee.

"Well, I was praying to God, and I was overcome with this feeling—this *knowledge*—I needed to do something of greater value in my life. I had been wondering if I should go into ministry, and God confirmed it right then and there. I gave up the prospect of marriage, wealth, and ownership of personal property. I went into ministry."

I then asked, "That was being baptized with the Holy Spirit?"

"It sure was."

"Could you help me understand what you believe baptism with the Holy Spirit is?" I asked. "Like, how could I recognize it if it happens to someone else, or how could I know if it was happening to me, as opposed to just feeling a wave of emotions?"

"Well, it's all semantics, isn't it?" Trevor said.

"What do you mean by that?" I asked

John and Lloyd worked on finishing their coffees while

listening to the conversation between Trevor and me. One thing I loved about Trevor and Lloyd was they were laid back, but they were also completely devoted to their work. It was evident every time we met together. They, like John and me, were not interested in arguing. They wanted to pursue peace through Bible study and conversation.

"You may call it emotions," Trevor said, "I call it baptism with the Holy Spirit. We don't like getting caught up in definitions."

I thought about that for a moment before saying, "Last week, we all agreed on the biblical definition and purpose of tongues."

Trevor and Lloyd nodded their heads.

"Well, what do you think about our friends in the Pentecostal movement who believe they are baptized with the Holy Spirit when they lose control of the body and speak in unintelligible speech? Should we boil our differences down to simple semantics?"

"Hmm…" Trevor thought. "I think I see what you're getting at."

"Instead of word games, can we look at baptism with the Holy Spirit in the New Testament a little closer?"

"Of course!"

The four of us opened our Bibles.

* * * * * * *

Many people share Trevor's tendency to dismiss matters when it comes to the details of the Holy Spirit and miracles. Some people claim it all amounts to word games. Is that true? Have I been too detail-oriented in this book? Does it make a difference how you or I word things? How much does it matter for someone to believe *exactly* as I believe when it comes to the Holy Spirit and miracles?

Notice how this chapter follows directly after a chapter where I admit I do not know the complete, detailed answer to an important question. I must always be open to the possibility that I am wrong. I must be willing to hear others out. I am not the standard. Nor is this book. Nor are your religious experiences. Nor are deeply devoted religious leaders. Nor are church manuals, Bible dictionaries, or religious creeds. God's will, revealed in the Scriptures, is the unmovable standard.

Do I know everything about the Holy Spirit and miracles? Impossible! Do I know everything the Scriptures tell us about the Holy Spirit and miracles? Far from it. But I have shared with you in this book what I have learned in my deep study. Judge for yourself. Have I taught the scriptural truth?

Words are important. I will assume you agree, since you have made it this far in this book, which is made up of *words*. Words are how anything exists, since God spoke everything into existence in the beginning through *words*. "The Word" is how Jesus Himself is known.[1]

However, having words in a perfect order is not always necessary to communicate God's message accurately. The gospel accounts themselves are the perfect example. Four chosen men— Matthew, Mark, Luke, and John—all tell us what Jesus "began to do and teach, until the day when He was taken up to heaven, after He had by the Holy Spirit given orders to the apostles whom He had chosen" (Acts 1:1–2). In telling us the same story, they used different arrangements of words to do so.

On the other hand, sometimes even the smallest detail in wording matters. For example, the apostle Paul explains God's plan to save man through His Son is found within semantics.

> *Now the promises were spoken to Abraham and to his seed. He does not say, "And to seeds," as referring to many, but rather to one, "And to your seed," that is, Christ.*
>
> *Galatians 3:16*

Is there a difference between the words *seed* and *seeds*? Hardly. Is that small difference a big deal? Only if you consider your redemption through the work of Jesus a big deal!

Where do we draw the line? Where can we say specific wording is not important on one subject; however, on another

---

[1] See John 1:1–14 and 1 John 1:1–4.

subject, we must agree on a single definition? The easy answer is this: When the Scriptures give us a definition, that settles it. When the Scriptures make the discernment for us, there is no room for our own. And the Scriptures have given us clear ways to understand who the Holy Spirit is, why He gave miraculous gifts, the specifics of those gifts, and how He is active in the lives of believers today.

In Acts 18, we read about Apollos, who is called "an eloquent man,...mighty in the Scriptures" (v. 24). He preached the gospel the best he could in Ephesus. However, his knowledge—and, therefore, his preaching—was incomplete.

> *This man had been instructed in the way of the Lord; and being fervent in spirit, he was speaking and teaching accurately the things concerning Jesus, being acquainted only with the baptism of John.*
>
> *Acts 18:25*

At this point, John's baptism had already passed its expiration date. When it was valid, it was practiced in preparation for the coming Messiah. Jesus' redemptive work is now complete, and He now commands a new baptism—one that associates a person with Christ's death, burial, and resurrection.

> *Or do you not know that all of us who have been baptized into Christ Jesus have been baptized into His death? Therefore we have been buried with Him through baptism into death, so that as Christ was raised from the dead through the glory of the Father, so we too might walk in newness of life. For if we have become united with Him in the likeness of His death, certainly we shall also be in the likeness of His resurrection.*
>
> *Romans 6:3–5*

When Priscilla and Aquila, a couple of faithful disciples, heard Apollos' incomplete preaching, "they took him aside and explained to him the way of God more accurately" (Acts 18:26). The problem was Apollos' understanding of baptism was inaccurate. Just a few verses later, we read:

> *It happened that while Apollos was at Corinth, Paul passed*

through the upper country and came to Ephesus, and found some disciples. He said to them, "Did you receive the Holy Spirit when you believed?" And they said to him, "No, we have not even heard whether there is a Holy Spirit." And he said, "Into what then were you baptized?" And they said, "Into John's baptism." Paul said, "John baptized with the baptism of repentance, telling the people to believe in Him who was coming after him, that is, in Jesus." When they heard this, they were baptized in the name of the Lord Jesus.

Acts 19:1–5

These men had likely listened to Apollos' preaching, which resulted in their participation in the wrong baptism. Apollos had already left town.[2] What would have happened if Paul had not passed through Ephesus, met these men, and corrected them? They were sincere, yet they were sincerely wrong. They knew nothing of the Holy Spirit. They would have carried on believing falsehood, presumably teaching it to others, baptizing them into the wrong baptism, and birthing the next generation of what would have amounted to a false religion.

Upon meeting them and learning about their knowledge and experiences, Paul does not deride them. He does not question their sincerity. He does not make fun of their religious experiences. However, there was a problem with the way they understood things, and he was not too shy to correct them. The same goes for how Priscilla and Aquila approached Apollos.

If this were to happen today, perhaps Apollos and these men from Ephesus would have chalked it all up to word games. "Look, Paul, you say we need to be baptized one way, yet we had a different religious experience. Who are you to emphasize one way of thinking over another? It's just semantics. God knows our hearts."

About a decade later, the same apostle would write to Christians in the same area:

---

[2] See Acts 18:27–28.

> *Therefore I, the prisoner of the Lord, implore you to walk in a manner worthy of the calling with which you have been called, with all humility and gentleness, with patience, showing tolerance for one another in love, being diligent to preserve the unity of the Spirit in the bond of peace. There is one body and one Spirit, just as also you were called in one hope of your calling; one Lord, one faith, one baptism, one God and Father of all who is over all and through all and in all.*
>
> *Ephesians 4:1–6*

How important is it we understand the Spirit the same way? How important is it we understand baptism similarly? As important as unity is to Jesus. When Paul begged the Christians in Ephesus to "preserve the unity of the Spirit," he used both the Holy Spirit and baptism as subjects on which they should be unified, since there is only *one* Spirit and *one* baptism. But it will take patience and tolerance. Hear Jesus' prayer on the eve of His death:

> *Sanctify them in the truth; Your word is truth. As You sent Me into the world, I also have sent them [the apostles] into the world. For their sakes I sanctify Myself, that they themselves also may be sanctified in truth. I do not ask on behalf of these alone, but for those also who believe in Me through their word; that they may all be one; even as You, Father, are in Me and I in You, that they also may be in Us, so that the world may believe that You sent Me. The glory which You have given Me I have given to them, that they may be one, just as We are one; I in them and You in Me, that they may be perfected in unity, so that the world may know that You sent Me, and loved them, even as You have loved Me.*
>
> *John 17:17–23*

There are two events in Scripture that are identified as baptism with the Holy Spirit. These events were separated by more than seven years. Considering that, is it acceptable for me to now start labelling religious experiences with different circumstances, descriptions, and purposes as "baptism with the Holy Spirit"? No.

And He said to them, "Rightly did Isaiah prophesy of you hypocrites, as it is written: 'This people honors Me with their lips, but their heart is far away from Me. But in vain do they worship Me, teaching as doctrines the precepts of men. Neglecting the commandment of God, you hold to the tradition of men.'"

Mark 7:6–8

The gift of tongues in the Scriptures is clearly explained as a gift of real, understandable languages for a specific purpose. When someone near me unexplainedly starts speaking in what amounts to gibberish, is it acceptable for me to say that person has the gift of tongues from the Holy Spirit? No.

Whatever you do in word or deed, do all in the name of the Lord Jesus, giving thanks through Him to God the Father.

Colossians 3:17

My friends in the Jehovah's Witness religion call the Holy Spirit a non-living force. Yet the Holy Spirit in the Scriptures loves your soul deeply and has gone to miraculous measures to provide the gospel to you. Is it just word games for someone to say God Almighty is an "it"? By no means!

Let us strive to look at the Scriptures together to give glory to God *together*.

*Now may the God who gives perseverance and encouragement grant you to **be of the same mind with one another according to Christ Jesus,** so that with one accord you may with one voice glorify the God and Father of our Lord Jesus Christ.*

Romans 15:5–6

*Now I exhort you, brethren, by the name of our Lord Jesus Christ, **that you all agree** and that there be no divisions among you, but that you **be made complete in the same mind and in the same judgment**.*

1 Corinthians 1:10

If we go on insisting that our religious experiences can define scriptural words, how can we "all agree" and "be made complete in the same mind and in the same judgment"? How can we diligently seek "the unity of the Spirit" if our understanding of the Spirit Himself is what divides us?

I have studied these things and have gone to great measures to explain them to you the way I understand the Scriptures to teach. I'm truly convicted of these things. But my eyes, heart, mind, and ears will always be open. Let us remember neither this book, nor any man-made book, will ever be the authority on these matters. If I have misspoken, and you are willing to approach me about it with the truth of the Scriptures, you have my promise to listen. This is not about me. It is about Him.

He must increase, but I must decrease.

John 3:30

There is a lot more to learn. Keep studying. Keep serving. Keep praying. Let us keep the charge of Jude 20–21 together.

But you, beloved, building yourselves up on your most holy faith, praying in the Holy Spirit, keep yourselves in the love of God, waiting anxiously for the mercy of our Lord Jesus Christ to eternal life.

NOW WHAT?

It truly is unfortunate that many people's understanding of the Holy Spirit has been clouded by emotion and a book such as this has had to spend so much time addressing false teachings on the Holy Spirit and miracles. But I suppose it is not much different than it was in the first century. Much of the New Testament was written to address false teachings or false teachers. Jude admits that when he planned to write to the Christians, his original intention was to write "about our common salvation" (Jude 3). Instead, he had to exhort the Christians to fight for the faith. Why?

For certain persons have crept in unnoticed, those who were long beforehand marked out for this condemnation, ungodly persons who turn the grace of our God into licentiousness and deny our only Master and Lord, Jesus Christ.

Jude 4

But once the falsehood was addressed, the praises began.

> *Now to Him who is able to keep you from stumbling, and to make you stand in the presence of His glory blameless with great joy, to the only God our Savior, through Jesus Christ our Lord, be glory, majesty, dominion and authority, before all time and now and forever. Amen.*
>
> Jude 24–25

Similar constructions can be found in the writings of Peter, Paul, and John. I am certainly not inspired the way these men were, but maybe we can adopt their strategy. Paul ends his letter to the Romans like this:

> *Now I urge you, brethren, keep your eye on those who cause dissensions and hindrances contrary to the teaching which you learned, and turn away from them. For such men are slaves, not of our Lord Christ but of their own appetites; and by their smooth and flattering speech they deceive the hearts of the unsuspecting. For the report of your obedience has reached to all; therefore I am rejoicing over you, but I want you to be wise in what is good and innocent in what is evil. The God of peace will soon crush Satan under your feet. The grace of our Lord Jesus be with you.*
>
> Romans 16:17–20

The falsehood has been dealt with. Hopefully you and I have both turned away from those who teach contrary to the word of Christ. Now, as our minds are no longer clouded, we can proceed to love God with all of our heart, soul, strength, and mind.

> *Praise God, from whom all blessings flow;*
> *Praise Him, all creatures here below;*
> *Praise Him above, ye heavenly host;*
> *Praise Father, Son, and Holy Ghost. Amen.*[3]

---

[3] Ken, Thomas. Final lines of the hymn, "Awake, My Soul, and With the Sun." 1674.

DISCUSSION QUESTIONS

1. What is one example of when specific wording is unimportant to teaching and relating to others?

2. What is one example of when specific wording is important to teaching and relating to others?

3. Why was it important for Priscilla, Aquila, and Paul to correct those who had the wrong understanding of the Holy Spirit and baptism?

4. How can we know when specific wording is important to God?

5. How important is "the unity of the Spirit" to God? How important is it to you?

6. What stood out to you as particularly interesting or helpful in this chapter?

7. How does this study help you approach God with greater reverence?

DEEPER DEVOTION
www.cloudedbyemotion.com

APPENDIX
ARE WE SAVED BY FAITH ALONE?

My ears were ringing, but it was worth it. I had been waiting to see that band in concert for years. When they finally came to Nashville, I couldn't pass up the opportunity.

It was normal to see people outside of concert venues handing things out as the mad exodus made for the parking lots. They were usually handing out flyers for upcoming concerts or demo discs from local bands. I was always keen to hear new music, so I grabbed whatever I could.

Walking to my car, I started to read what a middle-aged man had given me. "If you die tonight, will you go to heaven or hell?" *This isn't a flyer; it's a tract!*

I knew the answer though. Heaven was my eternal home. I knew that, not by some feeling in my heart, and not because some religious leader told me so, but because of the promise of God in what was written.[1]

I turned the tract over, and I saw a familiar, but heart-breaking sight.

> If you are ready to receive Jesus Christ as your Lord and Savior and be sure you will go to heaven, pray this prayer: "Dear Lord, I know I am a sinner in need of Your forgiveness. I now place my faith in You, accept You as my personal Lord and Savior, and invite You to come into my heart and forgive me of my sins. In Your name, Amen."

After the prayer on the tract, there was an encouragement for the "newly born again" person to seek out a Bible-believing church.

---

[1] See 1 John 5:13.

* * * * * * *

I want to be sensitive, but this type of teaching has coaxed millions of people into the mouth of the roaring lion, the devil. Will a simple prayer lead someone to heaven? Will "faith alone" save a person? What do the Scriptures say?

MY DISCLAIMER

I understand that salvation offered in Christ is the most precious gift.[2] I will do my best to be both sincere and sensitive. If I challenge your belief system in this appendix, I do not do so maliciously. I am doing my best to present the "simplicity and purity of devotion to Christ" (2 Corinthians 11:3). If you believe I miss the mark, I would be happy to hear you out, as I take James 3:1–11 seriously.

BASICS

If you were to be brave enough to ask your friends or local religious leaders, "What must I do to be saved?" what answers do you think you would receive? One of the most popular responses these days is, "Just believe in the Lord Jesus, and you will be saved." Is that biblical? Almost. In fact, that is *almost* a direct quotation of a passage in the Bible (more on that later).

This answer comes from those who sincerely teach salvation by faith alone. Although it is extremely popular today, "Just believe," is a fairly new answer to questions about salvation. In fact, you would be hard-pressed to find anyone teaching a faith-alone salvation before the 1500s.

To make a long history lesson short, the faith-alone doctrine stems from a movement ignited by Martin Luther and other men against the unscriptural teachings of the Roman Catholic Church of the 1500s.[3] Huldrych Zwingli (1484–1531) was the first well-known theologian who started teaching salvation by faith alone. By his own admission, he went against almost 1,500

---

[2] See Ephesians 2:8.
[3] As damaging as the faith alone doctrine is, I feel compelled to mention how thankful I am for the boldness of Martin Luther. His work opened many doors of religious freedom that many people enjoy today.

years of Bible teachings and beliefs when he taught salvation by faith alone, claiming that teachers "have been in error since the apostles."[4]

Whether we are saved by faith alone or not is most relevant these days when the question of baptism comes up. For instance, if one has been taught salvation is by faith alone, and he encounters Mark 16:16, he might become confused. In this verse, Jesus says:

> *He who has believed and has been baptized shall be saved; but he who has disbelieved shall be condemned.*

The doctrine of faith alone is quite simple, really. It teaches as soon as you believe in your heart Jesus died for your sins and rose again, you are saved, forgiven, and granted eternal life.[5] This "faith" would exclude all "works," including obedience.[6]

When faith alone began circulating in the Christian communities, many who trusted in the doctrine to save them came out of their experience lacking something. They felt a bit overwhelmed with emotion and underwhelmed with confirmation. In order to develop a reference point, people started practicing the Sinner's Prayer, which was what was on the back of the tract I received.

There is a major problem with the Sinner's Prayer. It is not in Scripture. More and more people are starting to realize that.

---

[4] Bromiley, G. W., ed. *Zwingli and Bullinger.* Westminster John Knox Press, 1953, 119–175.

[5] This is how advocates of faith alone have typically presented the doctrine to me in conversation. There are variants of the doctrine, so if you're ever in conversation with people who believe in faith alone, I recommend you ask them what they mean by "faith alone," instead of assuming what they believe.

[6] Though baptism is never referred to as a "work" in Scripture, proponents of faith alone frequently call it a work. In reality, when the apostles and prophets speak of salvation apart from works (e.g. Ephesians 2:8–9), context shows us that the "works" are works of the Law of Moses, not the commandments of Jesus. "For we maintain that a man is justified by faith *apart from works of the Law*" (Romans 3:28). In reality, the "washing of regeneration" is clearly distinguished from "deeds which we have done in righteousness" (Titus 3:5), and that which is accomplished at baptism is "through faith in *the working of God*" (Colossians 2:12), not in the work of the one being baptized.

Though unscriptural, the Sinner's Prayer is convenient. It gives the "new believer" a reference point. The doctrine of faith alone leaves the moment of conversion unknown; whereas, the contradictory "faith alone *plus* the Sinner's Prayer" successfully provides a dot on a timeline.

It is possible to know one is saved and to point to a moment in time when forgiveness occurs. It is not based on feelings or a declaration by some religious leader or tract. It is based on what has been written. Can you compare and equate your "salvation experience" with the Scriptures?

> *These things I have **written** to you who believe in the name of the Son of God, **so that you may know** that you have eternal life.*
>
> *1 John 5:13*

WHO WILL WIN THE FIGHT?

It really is sad that a significant number of those who profess a belief in the Bible do not give the same answer to the question, "What must I do to be saved?" Instead of going out and showing the scriptural answer to those desperately needing it, they argue amongst themselves how to answer it.

Unfortunately, once people become caught up in the argument, they are shoved into extreme categories like boxers in a ring. Each person must defend one side and offend the other side. "In the blue corner: Faith. In the red corner: Obedience. Round one, fight!" Then, one side brings all of the passages that only mention faith to the fight. The other side is forced to bring all of the passages that mention obedience or baptism. The one with the most Scriptures in the end wins. Is that how we are to treat God's word?

If you have ever participated in such a fight, you have effectively communicated God does not always mean what He says and it is okay to only believe part of the Scriptures. I am convinced, however, "*All* Scripture is inspired by God" (2 Timothy 3:16), who is a God who cannot lie and does not confuse.[7] Therefore, God meant what He said in all of the verses without contradiction. It is consistent and wonderfully liberating to believe *all* of the passages in the Scriptures about faith and *all* of the passages on obedience. Therefore, when I read our sins are washed away by the blood of Christ in Revelation 1:5, and we are saved by grace through faith in Ephesians 2:8, then I conclude blood, grace, and faith are connected to salvation. It is not blood alone. It is not grace alone. It is not faith alone. The truth is, if you actually search for the phrase "faith alone" in the Bible, you will find it only once.

> *You see that a man is justified by works and **not by faith alone.***
>
> *James 2:24*

Since this is the only passage that includes "faith alone," and it says we cannot be justified by faith alone, perhaps we need to seriously re-evaluate this popular doctrine.

WE ARE SAVED BY FAITH

Yes, it's true we are saved by faith, but not faith alone. First, Christ had to do the redemptive work. Without the shedding of Christ's blood, there would be no forgiveness of sins.[8] In order for us to hope in resurrection, He had to be the first fruits of an eternal life after death.[9] His work of redemption demands a response from us. He will not force us to be saved, but salvation is a gift to either be accepted or rejected.[10]

As far as being saved by the blood of Christ goes, we cannot look for examples in the four gospel accounts (Matthew, Mark, Luke, and John), since those cover the life and redemptive work of Christ. Those saved during the life of Christ were saved under the Law of Moses.[11] To begin looking at how one responds to the gift of salvation under the new covenant of Christ, we have to

---

[7] See Titus 1:2 and 1 Corinthians 14:33.
[8] See Hebrews 9.
[9] See 1 Corinthians 15.
[10] See Romans 6:23 and Hebrews 2:1–4.
[11] See Hebrews 9:15–17.

begin with the book of Acts.

When reading through this history book, we will see people encounter the gospel of Jesus' death and resurrection for the first time. The faith we see in the first disciples was not a superficial faith, but it transformed their entire lives and dictated their actions, similar to how those of the Old Testament responded to God.

> *Now faith is the assurance of things hoped for, the conviction of things not seen. For by it the men of old gained approval.*
>
> *Hebrews 11:1–2*

When we have true faith, we believe in a God powerful enough to speak the world into existence and always keep His promises—promises of both eternal life and condemnation. Therefore, to respond to God, we obey Him.

> *He who has My commandments and keeps them is the one who loves Me; and he who loves Me will be loved by My Father, and I will love him and will disclose Myself to him.*
>
> *John 14:21*

Much of the New Testament expresses the gift that Christians have "by grace…through faith" (Ephesians 2:8). We do not deserve anything but death, yet God still offers the gift of salvation.

> *For the wages of sin is death, but the free gift of God is eternal life in Christ Jesus our Lord.*
>
> *Romans 6:23*

Read the following passage while keeping in mind the book of Ephesians was written to those who have already been saved and come in contact with the blood of Christ.

> *For by grace you have been saved through faith; and that not of yourselves, it is the gift of God; not as a result of works, so that no one may boast. For we are His workmanship, created in Christ Jesus for good works, which God prepared beforehand so that we would walk in*

them.

Ephesians 2:8–10

The only proper way to respond to God's gift of grace and promise of judgment is by a working faith.

- By faith Abel offered (Hebrews 11:4).
- By faith Noah prepared (Hebrews 11:7).
- By faith Abraham obeyed and he went out (Hebrews 11:8).
- By faith Abraham looked for a city (Hebrews 11:10).
- By faith Abraham offered up Isaac (Hebrews 11:17).
- By faith Moses refused to be called the son of Pharaoh's daughter (Hebrews 11:24).
- By faith Moses chose to suffer affliction (Hebrews 11:25).
- By faith Moses forsook Egypt (Hebrews 11:27).
- By faith Moses kept the Passover (Hebrews 11:28).

There is a difference between earning our salvation (a concept utterly despised in Scripture) and fulfilling conditions God has placed on salvation. Just as the above cloud of witnesses exemplify, God expects us to respond to Him through faithful obedience, trusting He will fulfill His promises to those who endure until the end.

That is why people in the book of Acts responded to Christ in obedience immediately after they believed "the good news about the kingdom of God and the name of Jesus Christ" (Acts 8:12). When they saw the righteousness of Christ, they were willing to turn away from sin and turn toward God in repentance, trusting in the work of Jesus. They were also willing to bury the old person of sin through water baptism and allow the Spirit of God to raise them to walk in newness of life and transform them. Consider one example now.

As mentioned above, "Just believe in the Lord Jesus, and you will be saved" is *almost* a direct quotation from Scripture. In the biblical text, however, the word "just" is missing. In Acts 16, Paul and Silas were beaten and imprisoned. Instead of blaming God for the situation, they "were praying and singing hymns of praise to God, and the prisoners were listening to them" (v. 25). After a work of God shook him up (literally—there was an earthquake!), their jailer asked the most important question. Notice the question, the answer, and what follows.

> *And he called for lights and rushed in, and trembling with fear he fell down before Paul and Silas, and after he brought them out, he said, "Sirs, what must I do to be saved?" They said, "Believe in the Lord Jesus, and you will be saved, you and your household." And they spoke the word of the Lord to him together with all who were in his house. And he took them that very hour of the night and washed their wounds, and immediately he was baptized, he and all his household. And he brought them into his house and set food before them, and rejoiced greatly, having believed in God with his whole household.*
>
> *Acts 16:29–34*

After hearing these devout men's praise to God, this Roman, likely an idolatrous one, wanted to know the answer to the most important question he could ever ask. Unfortunately, many people rip verse 31 out of its context. When it is read in its context, however, we see the story in its entirety. In order for the jailer and his household to have true faith in Jesus, Paul and Silas had to speak "the word of the Lord" to him and his household. Then, the jailer washed Paul and Silas' wounds. If these wounds were dealt by his own hands, I can think of no better fruit of repentance. Though repentance was not mentioned specifically, I cannot imagine this man going back to his old way of life after knowing what Christ was willing to go through in order to wash his sins away. Then, "immediately he was baptized, he and all his household." After their baptisms, the household was rejoicing, "having believed in God." What do we learn from all of this? The jailer and his household were able to rejoice and were considered believers only after they heard the word of the Lord and were baptized into Christ.

People in the New Testament responded with faith in Christ immediately by dying to sin and being baptized into Christ. If you were to ask a first-century Christian when he was saved—at the point he believed in his heart, or at the point he was baptized—he would likely respond with a question of his own: "Huh?" Since conviction of sin, understanding of the gospel of Jesus, and being baptized into Christ happened "immediately" and "in the same hour," initial faith, repentance, and baptism were always considered to happen and work together. Unfortunately, since the 1500s, people have been trying to rip them apart.

Romans 6 teaches us baptism is the point at which a person crucifies and buries the old person of sin. Imagine a person learns about the gospel of Christ, and then repents by dying to sin, but then waits a year to be baptized. That entire year, he is a dead man walking! That man needs to bury his old person of sin and be raised to walk in newness of life!

> *What shall we say then? Are we to continue in sin so that grace may increase? May it never be! How shall we who died to sin still live in it? Or do you not know that all of us who have been baptized into Christ Jesus have been baptized into His death? Therefore we have been buried with Him through baptism into death, so that as Christ was raised from the dead through the glory of the Father, so we too might walk in newness of life. For if we have become united with Him in the likeness of His death, certainly we shall also be in the likeness of His resurrection, knowing this, that our old self was crucified with Him, in order that our body of sin might be done away with, so that we would no longer be slaves to sin; for he who has died is freed from sin.*
>
> *Romans 6:1–7*

The sum of Scripture is truth. Do you believe all of the verses on faith and all of the verses on obedience? It is abundantly clear in Scripture that the just reward for disobedience is death and eternal separation from God.[12] The only thing sinners have earned is their eternal destruction. That is why God freely offered salvation to us by His grace in the first place. How else

---

[12] See Romans 6:23.

should we respond to God's glorious gift, other than true, faithful love?

> *If you love Me, you will keep My commandments.*
>
>> John 14:15

> *...how will we escape if we neglect so great a salvation? After it was at the first spoken through the Lord, it was confirmed to us by those who heard...*
>
>> Hebrews 2:3

> *He who has believed and has been baptized shall be saved; but he who has disbelieved shall be condemned.*
>
>> Mark 16:16

No, Jesus does not say, "He who believes and says the Sinner's Prayer shall be saved." He says, "He who believes and has been baptized shall be saved."

Reaching for one last objection, I can already hear someone say, "But it only says, 'He who disbelieves shall be condemned,' not, 'He who is not baptized!'" That is absolutely true, but are we not interested in how to be *saved*, rather than being *condemned*? No person is going to choose to die to sin and be buried with Christ in baptism if he does not believe Christ can save him. How does Jesus say one can be *saved* in this passage?

SOME QUESTIONS

If you have been taught faith alone your entire life, I do not expect this single appendix, as long as it may be, to change your mind. My challenge to you would be to read the entire New Testament, watching for how people were forgiven by the blood of Christ. Don't read pockets of Scripture. Don't read single verses. Read it all.

> *As a result, we are no longer to be children, tossed here and there by waves and carried about by every wind of doctrine, by the trickery of men, by craftiness in deceitful scheming; but speaking the truth in love, we are to grow up in all aspects into Him who is the head, even Christ.*
>
>> Ephesians 4:14–15

Below are some questions that cannot be answered by faith alone without contradicting its own teaching or contradicting the Scriptures.

Are we not saved by the blood of Jesus?

One of the arguments that comes up frequently among faith alone proponents is the amount of passages that link faith and salvation together with no other condition explicitly mentioned. For instance, Acts 16:31 states:

> *They said, "Believe in the Lord Jesus, and you will be saved, you and your household."*

This is the perfect verse for pulling out of context and using to teach faith alone, since the jailer was told to believe. The logic is presented: Since faith is mentioned, and baptism is not, baptism is not necessary for salvation. However, with that logic, we are not saved by the blood of Jesus, since the redemptive blood is not mentioned in this verse. Beyond that, the jailer was permitted to continue living in sin, since repentance is not mentioned in this verse either.

Using this same method, one could use a number of verses to teach any number of "salvation by x alone" doctrines. For instance, we could teach repentance alone from 2 Corinthians 7:10, baptism alone from Acts 22:16, the life of Christ alone from Romans 5:10, the blood of Christ alone from Revelation 1:5, the word of God alone from James 1:21, obedience alone from Hebrews 5:9, and so on.

> *The sum of Your word is truth,*
> *And every one of Your righteous ordinances is everlasting.*
> *Psalm 119:160*

As a side note, I have recently heard a few preachers say the contradictory statement, "You are saved by grace alone by faith alone." If it is grace alone, faith cannot be included, since it is grace *alone*. The same is true if it is faith alone. Grace must be excluded. As the psalmist states, the sum of God's word is truth. However, when we make passages fight against each other, we are saying only *some* of God's word is truth.

What healed the blind man?

> *As He passed by, He saw a man blind from birth. And His disciples asked Him, "Rabbi, who sinned, this man or his parents, that he would be born blind?" Jesus answered, "It was neither that this man sinned, nor his parents; but it was so that the works of God might be displayed in him. We must work the works of Him who sent Me as long as it is day; night is coming when no one can work. While I am in the world, I am the Light of the world." When He had said this, He spat on the ground, and made clay of the spittle, and applied the clay to his eyes, and said to him, "Go, wash in the pool of Siloam" (which is translated, Sent). So he went away and washed, and came back seeing.*
>
> John 9:1–7

Did the water heal the man? Could any blind person apply spittle and clay to his eyes and wash in the pool of Siloam and be healed? No. It was not the physical elements, but Jesus who healed the blind man. However, would the blind man have been healed if he was unwilling to go to the water? The passage says, "So he went away and washed, and came back seeing" (John 9:7). If this man were listed in Hebrews 11, it would say, "By faith he went and washed in the pool." He would not have been healed if he had not washed, since it was a condition Christ put on his healing. When the critics came, they did not criticize the water; they criticized the Healer. Though it was necessary for his healing, the formerly blind man did not give credit to the pool for his health. Speaking of Christ, he said, "*He* opened my eyes" (John 9:30). However, even this man recognized washing was part of the process.

> *He answered, "The man who is called Jesus made clay, and anointed my eyes, and said to me, 'Go to Siloam and wash'; so I went away and washed, and I received sight."*
>
> John 9:11

The water was necessary, but the power was not in the water; it was in the Healer. Likewise, the teaching of baptismal regeneration, (which, depending on who is teaching it, sometimes means baptism by itself will save someone) is utterly false. However, Christ put baptism as a condition of one's salvation, along with belief and repentance. When Jesus fulfills His promise of "He who has believed and has been baptized shall be saved," it would make no sense to give praise to the water. All credit is due to the Healer of the soul, who always keeps His promises.

What will become of those who only call Jesus "Lord"?

I've seen Romans 10:13 listed to validate the Sinner's Prayer. It says:

> for "Whoever will call on the name of the Lord will be saved."

However, if this passage means to say all you have to do is verbally call Christ "Lord," it contradicts Jesus' words elsewhere.

> Not everyone who says to Me, "Lord, Lord," will enter the kingdom of heaven, but he who does the will of My Father who is in heaven will enter. Many will say to Me on that day, "Lord, Lord, did we not prophesy in Your name, and in Your name cast out demons, and in Your name perform many miracles?" And then I will declare to them, "I never knew you; depart from Me, you who practice lawlessness."
>
> Matthew 7:21–23

How powerful, yet how terrifying! It is proper to call Jesus our Lord;[13] however, those who depend merely on that will be sorely surprised on the day of judgment. Instead, we must be found "clothed...with Christ" (Galatians 3:26–28) and "in the Lord" (Revelation 14:13) while we "walk in the light" (1 John 1:5–10).

> Why do you call Me, "Lord, Lord," and do not do what I say?
>
> Luke 6:46
>
> Now why do you delay? Get up and be baptized, and wash

---

[13] See John 13:13.

> *away your sins, calling on His name.*
>
> *Acts 22:16*

The above verse demonstrates that responding to the gospel through baptism *is* calling on the Lord's name. Likewise, all aspects of "everyone who calls on the name of the Lord will be saved" in Acts 2:21 can also be found in the commandment a few verses later: "Repent, and each of you be baptized in the name of Jesus Christ for the forgiveness of your sins" (Acts 2:38). Everyone/each of you; call on the name of the Lord/be baptized in the name of Jesus Christ; will be saved/for the forgiveness of your sins.

What about those who die outside of the Lord?

While reading through Paul's writings, it is hard to miss his frequent references to blessings found in Christ. For instance, eternal life, forgiveness of sins, and salvation are all found "in Christ."[14]

> *Therefore if anyone is in Christ, he is a new creature; the old things passed away; behold, new things have come.*
>
> *2 Corinthians 5:17*

The apostle John also shows us the imagery of someone being in the Lord.

> *And I heard a voice from heaven, saying, "Write, 'Blessed are the dead who die in the Lord from now on!'" "Yes," says the Spirit, "so that they may rest from their labors, for their deeds follow with them."*
>
> *Revelation 14:13*

Those who die in the Lord are blessed. This is in contrast to those who die in their sins.[15] The question remains, then, how are we placed into Christ? How are we transferred from being in our sins to being in the Lord?

> *For you are all sons of God through faith in Christ Jesus. For all of you who were baptized into Christ have clothed*

---

[14] See Romans 6:23; Colossians 1:13–14; and 2 Timothy 2:10.
[15] See John 8:24.

> *yourselves with Christ. There is neither Jew nor Greek,*
> *there is neither slave nor free man, there is neither male*
> *nor female; for you are all one in Christ Jesus.*
>
> *Galatians 3:26–28*[16]

The way to be placed into Christ is through faithful obedience to Christ in baptism. To say that we do not need to be baptized to receive Christ's salvation is to say that we can be saved outside of Christ and without eternal life, forgiveness of sins, or eternal salvation, since those blessings are found only in Christ.

How can one be saved outside of the body of Christ?

It is common today to try to have a "relationship with Jesus Christ" without being associated with His church. That is scripturally impossible. In the New Testament, the church was made up of the saved, and the saved made up the church.[17]

> *And He put all things in subjection under His feet, and*
> *gave Him as head over all things to the church, which is*
> *His body, the fullness of Him who fills all in all.*
>
> *Ephesians 1:22–23*

> *For the husband is the head of the wife, as Christ also is the*
> *head of the church, He Himself being the Savior of the*
> *body.*
>
> *Ephesians 5:23*

Jesus is the Savior of His body, the church. As above, if you were to ask a first-century Christian, "Did you become saved first, or did you become a part of the church first?" he would likely respond with his own question: "Huh?" They happened at the same time, as Christ is "the Savior of the body." How does one enter the body of Christ?

> *For even as the body is one and yet has many members,*
> *and all the members of the body, though they are many,*
> *are one body, so also is Christ. For by one Spirit we were all*

---

[16] See also Romans 6:1–7 and 1 Corinthians 12:12–13.

[17] See Acts 2:40–47.

> baptized into one body, whether Jews or Greeks, whether
> slaves or free, and we were all made to drink of one Spirit.
>
> 1 Corinthians 12:12–13
>
> There is one body and one Spirit, just as also you were
> called in one hope of your calling; one Lord, one faith, one
> baptism, one God and Father of all who is over all and
> through all and in all.
>
> Ephesians 4:4–6

Those who teach salvation by faith alone offer a "salvation"
outside of the body of Christ and devoid of God's Spirit.

What about the demons?

In James 2, James explains to his audience that laziness in
Christ will not suffice. God expects His people to prove their
faith by making the world a better place.

> You believe that God is one. You do well; the demons also
> believe, and shudder. But are you willing to recognize, you
> foolish fellow, that faith without works is useless?
>
> James 2:19–20

I understand James is not teaching someone how to be saved.
He is writing to Christians, those who have already been saved.
However, to help prove his point that Christians should be
working for Christ, he says demons believe in God. Are those
who profess faith alone going to be consistent and teach demons
are saved?

What about the unrighteous?

Many people who teach salvation by faith alone teach as soon
as you believe in your heart, and before you repent of your sins,
you are forgiven.

> Or do you not know that the unrighteous will not inherit
> the kingdom of God? Do not be deceived; neither
> fornicators, nor idolaters, nor adulterers, nor effeminate,
> nor homosexuals, nor thieves, nor the covetous, nor
> drunkards, nor revilers, nor swindlers, will inherit the
> kingdom of God. Such were some of you; but you were
> washed, but you were sanctified, but you were justified in

> *the name of the Lord Jesus Christ and in the Spirit of our God.*
>
>   *1 Corinthians 6:9–11*

Paul boldly claims those living unrighteous lives will not inherit the kingdom of God. Doubtless, he was elated to be able to say, "Such *were* some of you." These Corinthians had changed their ways. God had washed them and given them a sanctified life in His Spirit, which, he explains a few chapters later, happened at their baptism.[18] Godly sorrow produces a repentance to salvation. Would those who teach faith alone also teach one can remain in his or her sins and be saved?

> *For the sorrow that is according to the will of God produces a repentance without regret, leading to salvation, but the sorrow of the world produces death.*
>
>   *2 Corinthians 7:10*
>
> *Peter said to them, "Repent, and each of you be baptized in the name of Jesus Christ for the forgiveness of your sins; and you will receive the gift of the Holy Spirit."*
>
>   *Acts 2:38*

Is love of any value?

Faith alone means just that. Faith and nothing else.

> *If I speak with the tongues of men and of angels, but do not have love, I have become a noisy gong or a clanging cymbal. If I have the gift of prophecy, and know all mysteries and all knowledge; and **if I have all faith, so as to remove mountains, but do not have love, I am nothing**. And if I give all my possessions to feed the poor, and if I surrender my body to be burned, but do not have love, it profits me nothing.*
>
>   *1 Corinthians 13:1–3*

Though not directly related to the salvation of the soul, this Scripture claims, "if I have all faith, so as to remove mountains, but do not have love, I am nothing." Meaning, in order for us to

---

[18] See 1 Corinthians 12:12–13.

amount for something in the eyes of God, we need at least faith *and* love. Faith alone will not cut it.

Is obedience irrelevant to salvation?

The *Standard Manual for Baptist Churches* claims:

> *Baptism is not essential to salvation, for our churches utterly repudiate the dogma of "baptismal regeneration"; but it is essential to obedience, since Christ has commanded it.*[19]

Salvation by baptism alone, which is what baptismal regeneration sometimes teaches, surely is false. On this, Edward Hiscox, the author of the manual, is correct. However, I cannot agree with his conclusion. Hiscox says Baptist churches believe obedience is not essential to salvation, which is the opposite of what the Holy Spirit teaches.

> *Although He was a Son, He learned obedience from the things which He suffered. And having been made perfect, He became to all those who obey Him the source of eternal salvation.*
>
> *Hebrews 5:8–9*
>
> *He who believes in the Son has eternal life; but he who does not obey the Son will not see life, but the wrath of God abides on him.*
>
> *John 3:36*

What will Christ really judge?

Faith alone claims Christ judges the soul by merely what the person holds in the heart. Examine the passages that actually explain how Christ will judge when He appears.

> *Then Jesus said to His disciples, "If anyone wishes to come after Me, he must deny himself, and take up his cross and follow Me. For whoever wishes to save his life will lose it; but whoever loses his life for My sake will find it. For what will it profit a man if he gains the whole world and forfeits*

---

[19] Hiscox, Edward Thurston. *The Standard Manual for Baptist Churches.* American Baptist Publication Society, 1903, 21.

*his soul? Or what will a man give in exchange for his soul? For the Son of Man is going to come in the glory of His Father with His angels, and will then repay every man **according to his deeds**."*

> Matthew 16:24–27

*There will be tribulation and distress for every soul of man who **does evil**, of the Jew first and also of the Greek, but glory and honor and peace to everyone **who does good**, to the Jew first and also to the Greek. For there is no partiality with God.*

> Romans 2:9–11

*Therefore we also have as our ambition, whether at home or absent, to be pleasing to Him. For we must all appear before the judgment seat of Christ, so that each one may be recompensed **for his deeds in the body, according to what he has done, whether good or bad**.*

> 2 Corinthians 5:9–10

*For after all it is only just for God to repay with affliction those who afflict you, and to give relief to you who are afflicted and to us as well when the Lord Jesus will be revealed from heaven with His mighty angels in flaming fire, dealing out retribution to **those who do not know God and to those who do not obey the gospel of our Lord Jesus**. These will pay the penalty of eternal destruction, away from the presence of the Lord and from the glory of His power.*

> 2 Thessalonians 1:6–9

Honestly, the number of passages that mentions deeds and works as they relate to judgment surprises me. There are dozens more not listed above. I encourage you to search them out yourself. Our response to God's free gift should be obedient, faithful love and reverence. Of course, this does not mean we earn our salvation by doing good deeds. Ephesians 2:8–10 and Romans 6:23 still hold true. However, to teach that deeds and works are irrelevant to eternal salvation and judgment would also be a mistake.

Where does the Bible say that?

The most common description of baptism that I have heard from faith alone proponents is baptism is "an outward symbol (or sign) of an inward salvation (or grace)." My question is simple: Where do the Scriptures say that? It cannot be found.

Baptism itself is nothing without faith in the subject's heart and the promises of God to back it up. There is nothing miraculous about water that can cleanse the soul by itself, otherwise, we should be busy grabbing all unbelievers and dunking them, even against their will. However, God has deemed baptism in water as the way He connects a person with the death, burial, and resurrection of Christ. That is the reference point that is lacking in "faith alone," which men have replaced with the Sinner's Prayer. Baptism is when God circumcises the heart without hands, when He forgives all transgressions, and when He raises up the person who has been granted a new life through the resurrection of Jesus.

> *And in Him you were also circumcised with a circumcision made without hands, in the removal of the body of the flesh by the circumcision of Christ; having been buried with Him in baptism, in which you were also raised up with Him through faith in the working of God, who raised Him from the dead. When you were dead in your transgressions and the uncircumcision of your flesh, He made you alive together with Him, having forgiven us all our transgressions.*
>
> *Colossians 2:11–13*
>
> *Corresponding to that* [the water that saved Noah and his family], *baptism now saves you—not the removal of dirt from the flesh, but an appeal to God for a good conscience—through the resurrection of Jesus Christ.*
>
> *1 Peter 3:21*

The fact that God works through the death, burial, and resurrection of Jesus during baptism is an important point to remember when conversing with people on this topic. The poster child of faith alone is the thief on the cross in Luke 23:39–43.

Some people claim he was promised paradise on the basis of his faith alone. However, no one knows whether or not the thief was ever baptized. Some assert he was likely baptized, as "all the country of Judea was going out to him [John], and all the people of Jerusalem; and they were being baptized by him" (Mark 1:5), yet we are still left guessing if this man was part of that group.

The more important point is Jesus did not command baptism in the name of the Father, the Son, and the Holy Spirit until after His resurrection (which was weeks after the thief in question entered paradise). Jesus waited to command this baptism, because it is what unites someone with His death, burial, and resurrection, and thus is when someone contacts the forgiving blood of the covenant, as we see in Romans 6:1–7. It would have been impossible for anyone—including the thief on the cross—to be baptized *into* the death, burial, and resurrection of Jesus Christ *without* the death, burial, and resurrection of Jesus Christ having already happened. The thief on the cross lived and died under the Old Testament system, not the gospel system.[20]

> *Or do you not know that all of us who have been baptized into Christ Jesus have been **baptized into His death?** Therefore we have been **buried with Him through baptism into death**, so that as Christ was raised from the dead through the glory of the Father, so we too might **walk in newness of life**. For if we have become united with Him in the likeness of His death, certainly we shall also be in the likeness of His resurrection, knowing this, that **our old self was crucified with Him**, in order that our body of sin might be done away with, so **that we would no longer be slaves to sin**; for he who has died is freed from sin.*
>
> *Romans 6:3–7*

Do you want to trust in a salvation that does not connect you with the death of Christ? If so, go ahead and trust in the man-made doctrine of faith alone and the Sinner's Prayer. Or would you like to trust in God's plan that says, "if we have become united with Him in the likeness of His death, certainly we shall

---

[20] See Hebrews 9:15–17.

also be in the likeness of His resurrection"? If that's what you want, I beg of you: *obey God today*!

If you have trusted in faith alone or the Sinner's Prayer to save you, I hope you have considered these passages carefully. I challenge you to go back to the Scriptures. Put down the commentaries and other man-made books (including this one). Don't look on the internet for your answers. Read the entire New Testament, and see what God has been saying all along. Once you do, do not hesitate to trust and obey Him.

> *Grace and peace be multiplied to you in the knowledge of God and of Jesus our Lord; seeing that His divine power has granted to us everything pertaining to life and godliness, through the true knowledge of Him who called us by His own glory and excellence.*
>
> *2 Peter 1:2–3*

CLOSING THOUGHTS AND
ACKNOWLEDGEMENTS

I sat back in my chair and clasped my hands behind my head. A smile slowly emerged on my face. *I'm finished*, I thought. After nearly a year of writing and prayer, I had finished my eight-lesson series on the Holy Spirit and miracles for the church in Porirua. On the following Sunday, I would deliver the final lesson of the series.

I shared preaching responsibilities with a few other men, so it took a while to make it through the series. Plus, certain occasions sometimes called for a break in the series, and I would preach on a different topic when one of my two or three times per month to preach came around. In addition to that, my family had a two-month trip to the United States in the middle of my delivery. There's no wonder why it seemed like finishing an eight-lesson series felt like such an accomplishment. If only I knew where it would take me.

My friend, Stan Mitchell, used to say, "Study your questions; preach your convictions." I had surely done that, and I preached with genuine enthusiasm. Though I was confident in my scriptural conclusions, not asking for feedback with this project was not an option for me. When dealing with a subject that is often clouded by emotion and approached with trepidation (if at all), I wanted to make sure, as a teacher, I was as careful as possible while teaching others. James warns:

> *Let not many of you become teachers, my brethren, knowing that as such we will incur a stricter judgment. For we all stumble in many ways. If anyone does not stumble in what he says, he is a perfect man, able to bridle the whole*

body as well.

James 3:1–2

Soon after warning that there are parts of Scripture that are difficult to understand, Peter exhorts his audience:

You therefore, beloved, knowing this beforehand, be on your guard so that you are not carried away by the error of unprincipled men and fall from your own steadfastness, but grow in the grace and knowledge of our Lord and Savior Jesus Christ. To Him be the glory, both now and to the day of eternity. Amen.

2 Peter 3:17–18

This gives us who teach the Scriptures a multi-faceted warning that what we are dealing with is no light matter (after all, we're dealing with the revealed will of an infinite God!), and there will be serious, eternal consequences for the one who approaches the teaching of Scripture casually. Yet we should also find comfort that when we strive with all of our might, God's revealed knowledge is available to us, and we can *grow* in it, as well as grow in His grace where we struggle or lack knowledge.

I still was not sure what I was going to do with the eight lessons once I had finished preaching through them. I felt that such a task merited more than simply filing them away. At the beginning of delivering each of the lessons, I would ask the congregation to listen carefully and take notes of anything they would like to discuss afterward. Many of the congregation did, and I made revisions to each lesson after I delivered it based on those conversations. What would be the point of those revisions if the lessons were finished after a single delivery?

I had prepared the lessons as manuscripts, using the Bible studies I had written for studying with Danny as the basis. I don't always preach from manuscripts, but I knew with a series on the Holy Spirit and miracles, I wanted each sentence to be plotted out and each word carefully chosen. As I saw it, skeletal outlines were too dangerous for this job.

As I neared the completion of preparing the lessons, I asked my mother-in-law, a woman known for her love for the truth and her keen eye for literature, if she would like to read through the manuscripts to help me clean them up a bit. She came back to me with invaluable insight. I had thought one day I could turn the manuscripts into scripts for a video series. I also casually asked her, "Do you think the lessons could work as online articles?"

"Absolutely," came the reply.

But then I thought, *Why stop there?* I laid the eight lessons out before me, and realized I had prepared over 40,000 words. *That's the foundation of a book!* The rest, as they say, is history—but not a history I want to gloss over.

After I had assembled the eight lessons into a word processor, edited them, chopped them into eleven pieces, written two more lessons, and completed an appendix, I sat back in my chair and clasped my hands behind my head. A smile slowly emerged on my face. *I'm finished*, I thought.

I started contacting some friends to see if they were interested in beta reading the book. Fourteen agreed to do so. Over the course of the next two weeks, I made countless revisions based on their feedback, all of them helping shape the book into an easier to digest piece of effective teaching literature. Once all reviews were in, and the last revision made, I sat back in my chair and clasped my hands—well, you get the picture by now.

There remained in me a feeling that I was being lazy, if not self-preserving. My proofreaders were my friends. And of the ones that were active in teaching others the Scriptures, I knew we already agreed on almost everything I had written. I needed to reach further. I needed this work to be challenged. So, I went to some online forums and found some more beta readers from many different backgrounds, including, using their own descriptions of themselves, a born-again believer, a devout Roman Catholic, a former Wiccan delivered by Jesus, and a female Pentecostal pastor. I expected their feedback on the book to be interesting, to say the least. And it was, and so much more! Perhaps this was the most helpful (and bravest) step in developing this book into a work of integrity.

But even then, I was not ready to stop. Next, I asked over a dozen full-time Bible teachers, preachers, elders, and university professors to look closely at the manuscript. They came back to me with help in understanding this topic on a much deeper level, employing knowledge of the Hebrew and Greek languages and overall understanding of the working and teaching of Scripture.

Perhaps you were not interested in the story of how those first eight lessons turned into the book you hold now. However, I felt compelled to share the story, if only to let my beta readers, proofreaders, peer reviewers, and editor know how much I appreciate them. If you were one of those, and you have read through the book once again, you must have noticed the impact your and others' comments have made.

Let me also acknowledge *you*, the reader. Books begin to see their value once they have been read. My friend, Doyle Bruce, once told me over a dinner conversation, "You must be careful when reading books. They are quite persuasive, and I have seen some solid men of the faith lose their convictions in the Scriptures over reading a single book." You too should respect that advice. Even an inspired, wise preacher had this to say:

> The Preacher sought to find delightful words and to write words of truth correctly. The words of wise men are like goads, and masters of these collections are like well-driven nails; they are given by one Shepherd. But beyond this, my son, be warned: the writing of many books is endless, and excessive devotion to books is wearying to the body. The conclusion, when all has been heard, is: fear God and keep His commandments, because this applies to every person. For God will bring every act to judgment, everything which is hidden, whether it is good or evil.
>
> Ecclesiastes 12:10–14

If you truly have experienced any kind of paradigm shift while reading *Clouded by Emotion*, my prayer is that you see things closer to how God sees them, you have repented where necessary, and you have left behind false ideas to adhere to scriptural conclusions. I know this book did not answer every question we could ask on the Holy Spirit and miracles. In fact, if you were truly engaged in studying the Scriptures, more questions likely arose during your study. Let me remind you of the twofold purpose of this book:

1. To provide non-exhaustive, yet solid, easy-to-understand, scriptural teachings on the person and work of the Holy Spirit.
2. To provide logical tools and information to refute false teachings regarding the person and work of the Holy Spirit.

You and I still may not agree on everything. I admit that much of what pertains to the Holy Spirit and miracles in Scripture is still mysterious to me. I would be skeptical of anyone who believes he has it all figured out. But I hope you concur I have presented a careful, Scripture-based view of the Holy Spirit and miracles.

I'm grateful for the dozens of friends, acquaintances, and strangers who took the time to beta read, proofread, and peer review this book. Your comments along the way have helped shape this book into what it is.

To Kristen, my wife with enduring patience: thank you.

* * * * * * *

Please turn a few pages for a special request.

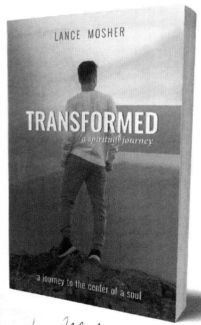
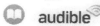

So, what did you think?

While it's fresh on your mind, will you please take a moment
to leave a review for *Clouded by Emotion*
on Amazon and other retailers?

Thank you for reading and reviewing!

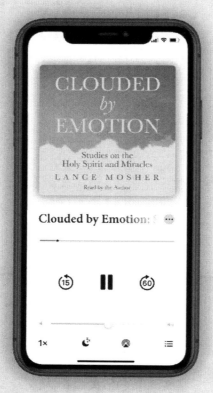

Audiobook also available.

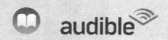

LanceMosherBOOKS.com
FOR YOUR JOURNEY

Made in the USA
Columbia, SC
14 February 2021